World Postmarks

BATSFORD STUDIES IN PHILATELY

Advisory editor: Arthur Blair FRPSL

R. K. Forster

WORLD
POSTMARKS

B. T. Batsford Ltd., London

First published 1973
© R. K. Forster 1973
0 7134 0382 9
Printed and bound in Great Britain by
C. Tinling & Co. Ltd,
Prescot, Lancashire
for the publishers
B. T. Batsford Ltd.,
4 Fitzhardinge Street London W1H OAH

To Heather
For May 6 1936 and
everything that followed

Contents

Contents

Line illustrations

Plates

Acknowledgement

The Author wishes to acknowledge his indebtedness to: The Director of the Bureau International de L'Union Postale Universelle, Berne, Switzerland, for information and statistical data; The Public Relations and Marketing Departments, The British Post Office, London; The Public Relations Department, The British Post Office, North East Region; The Director, Posts and Telegraphs, GPO, Sydney, Australia and Mr J. J. Olsen, Historical Officer, Postmaster-General's Department, GPO, Sydney, Australia, for practical help and advice; Arthur Blair, FRPSL, Consultant Editor, *Stamp Magazine*, and Mr R. M. Startup, FRPSNZ, Editor, *The Mail Coach* (New Zealand), for advisory assistance and help with the provision of illustrations.

The Author and Publishers also wish to thank W. & R. Chambers Limited and Stanley Paul and Company Limited for permission to quote passages from *The Postmark On A Letter* and *Postmark Collecting*; The Editors of *The Sunday Times*, *Yorkshire Post* and *Huddersfield Daily Examiner* for permission to quote extracts from their columns and to Miss Kathleen Partridge for generously allowing the use of a quotation from her poem in the series *Just A Thought*.

The author gratefully acknowledges the warm-hearted co-operation and helpfulness of fellow collectors, friends and officials in the postal services of many nations throughout the world who, for many years, have helped him to gather and present much of the material upon which this book is based.

Preface

For forty years I have been going round in circles—philatelic circles—collecting postmarks from places with unusual names and interesting background stories. It began in 1931 when a Sunday newspaper item about a place called Hell, in Norway, attracted my attention. I wondered if Hell had a post office. It had, and its postmark became one of the earliest 'believe it or not' place-names in my world-wide collection. (At that time, postally speaking, there was only one Hell on earth. Now there are two others: one in Michigan, USA, the other in the Cayman Islands.) Today my collection includes around 150,00 postmarks and covers—many of them from places with strange and fascinating tales to tell from every corner of the globe.

In my search for material I have touched down in many different countries, ranging from Alaska and Algeria to Japan, Thailand, Spain and Greece. Perhaps my deep personal involvement is not something about which I need to apologise although it will undoubtedly colour my approach to the subject. To me, a postmark is an authentic, often a dated, device with a personal story and a background into which it might be very well worthwhile to probe. Its shape, design and content have a tale to tell. It will certainly be worthy of close study. By means of it one can form reliable opinions about the routes taken in the conveyance of mail. Nothing about it should be taken for granted, and the part it plays in the miraculous chain of world communication will almost certainly have a background story of its own.

Let the reader think for a moment of his local post office and then compare its setting and its background with that of a post office in, say, Alaska, the Soviet Union, South America, Japan,

Australia or Pakistan. Again, the postmark may have links with some special event or a great occasion—perhaps even with the making of history; for postal history and postmarks are so intimately linked with everyday affairs.

With the postmark to focus one's interest, place-names begin to assume a new significance. How can one dismiss the promise of a name like Collywobbles, Bigbug or Wounded Knee? How did Total Wreck come by its name and why was a Lancashire locality called Mumps? What happened at Accident and why were Maggotty, Braggadocio and Bread Loaf so named? There is a post office in Uruguay called Treinta y Tres. In English that signifies Thirty-Three. With its postmark as the starting point one could uncover a dramatic and tragic story by pursuing such a name to its source. Beeswing, named for a famous racehorse, is the imprint of a village in Scotland. What link, if any, is there between this place and communities named Bee in Nebraska, Virginia and Italy and the strangely-named township of Bumble Bee in Arizona? Why was Lucky Strike so named and what curious circumstance gave to a post office in Umatilla county, Oregon, the extraordinary name Boiling Point? (Could it really have been because at this point, in hot weather, the old model-T Fords used to boil over and emit clouds of steam?)

These are tracks and highways along which the postmark on a letter may invite one to tread. Postmarks of this calibre have to be sought and found. They are well worth the search and the reward for finding them is to know that they are almost certainly authentic and real and had their beginning at the time and in the place whose date and details they bear.

Between postal markings and postal history there are obvious well-defined links. Few could resist the temptation to explore the origins of bygone material and in the realm of postal history much waits to be revealed. The aim of this book is to try to outline some of the ways in which an interest in postmarks can be awakened, developed and deployed. The serious collector will almost certainly wish to specialise in some region, theme, type or period. The beginner, on the other hand, may wish to feel his way: to explore; to survey the field and assess from the available material the branch of the hobby which he finds himself most drawn towards. That is why, in this survey, I have chosen to cover as wide a field as possible within the confines of a single volume.

Interest in postmarks and postal history has never been so great; accurate and purposeful research into the subject has never before been so widely undertaken. The output of monographs, handbooks and specialist studies has never been so prolific. In short, the hobby is booming on a world-wide scale. Interesting material can be acquired at modest cost on all levels and from many sources. As to the diversity and international scope of collectable material, I hope the pages of this book will indicate in a modest but reassuring way how vast and wide-ranging this is: in postmark collecting there are no frontiers; there are limitless horizons.

I
Looking Back

Many attempts have been made (and will no doubt continue in specialised fields) to trace postmarks back to their grass roots beginnings. It is a dificult research calling for much patience and scholarly skill.

Postal markings of one kind or another are said to have appeared on letters written 5,000 years ago by Egyptian Court officials in the time of the Third Dynasty. Examples of such markings in red and blue, on view in an Egyptian museum, show the place of the letters' origin and bear the exhortation 'In the name of the living King, speed!'

In February 1945 an ancient letter of the Babylonian era—c1900 BC—written or impressed on a baked brick, and relating to a business transaction and a debt, was offered as Lot 1 in a saleroom in London, England. The valuation then placed upon this rare item was £15. On offer in the same sale was a letter on water-marked paper written c1327 by Thomas, Cardinal of Naples, to the Archbishop of Salzburg. This item was described as a fine example of the period when the Roman Church had its own letter-carriers and it was conveyed at a time when the manufacture of paper of this standard was itself in its infancy.

The Romans organised Imperial postal services throughout their Empire and, later, letters deriving from the republic of Venice and from several of the small independent Italian states of the fourteenth and fifteenth centuries carried small circular marks identifiable as the forerunners of modern postmarks. Hand-written inscriptions, often specifying the vessel by which the letter was to be conveyed, are a feature of surviving sea-mail correspondence of this and later eras. Examples of many of these early impressions have survived on the letters of state officials and merchants; three such items—fifteenth-century letters from Venetia—when offered in an auction in England in the mid-1940s were valued at only £5. Since then prices have rocketed, as the chapter on postmark values will indicate.

Elsewhere in the world, as the demand for communication over wider areas became more pressing, separate states developed and operated postal services of varying standards. As they did so, many of them introduced rudimentary forms of postal markings, often in manuscript form. It is fascinating to trace these stages of development in different regions and so to begin a study of postal history.

In France the use of postmarks in a form recognisable as such today began about 1695. As early as 1700 receiving offices were functioning in such provincial centres as Granville and Saint-Hilaire-Du-Harcouet. One may choose to examine a specific region. For example, a study of Normandy would reveal the widening scope of postal markings ranging from the abbreviated handstamps of Saint-Lo and the diverse types of single-line town name strikes to the more elaborate handstamps incorporating departmental numerals and the lined rectangular date-stamps of 1828.

In the Austro-Hungarian Empire the first postmark to indicate the place of posting was used in Vienna in the autumn of 1751. The extent to which a single country can proliferate in its range of available material is instanced by the fact that in 1965 a specialist in Austrian cancellations estimated that some 10,000 different postmarks were in use in that country in 1870.

Across the world, in Mexico, cancellations of remarkable range and variety, in red, blue, green and yellow, made their appearance after the introduction of postage stamps in 1856. Many of the cancelling devices were made to the requirements of local postmasters and the resultant markings were often bizarre, picturesque and unusual in content and dimension.

In Russia, a state postal system using horse couriers was devised in the thirteenth century and had been organised on more sophisticated lines by the mid-seventeenth century. By 1913 some 7,620 official postal and telegraph establishments were functioning—contrasting with 72,000 post offices operating in 1966.

In 1641 the Duke of Brunswick inaugurated an internal postal service and after the introduction of postage stamps there in 1852, various types of cancellations began to appear, initially in the form of single-line markings and later in the shape of distinctive circular handstamps in blue or black, incorporating the place-name and the date and time of posting.

Sweden, an early entrant in the arena of communications, had a primitive form of internal postal service as early as the mid-sixteenth century. Its post office, one of the oldest in the world, was officially founded in 1636, but was actually in existence in 1620 when Gustavus II Adolphus established a mail route between Stockholm and Hamburg. But postmarks were not in use there until 1685; that is, 170 years before the appearance of the country's first postage stamps.

The Chinese Imperial Post Office, late in the field, produced an interesting 'Big Dollar Chop' cancellation at the turn of the nineteenth century.

In North America a postal service existed in 1639 and an early Federal post office was established in 1776 at 44 Corn Hill, Boston, Massachusetts. In the same year an office was opened in Ralston, New Jersey and Benjamin Franklin's ledger listed 82 offices in existence about this period. But handstamped postmarks were not widely used until the early 1860s. Around that time woodcuts or similar typeset cancellations were employed, often in the form of straight line town-names. A pioneer in this field was Edmond S. Zevely, postmaster of Pleasant Grove, Maryland, who manufactured handstamps for use in the United States.

In England, postmarks made their appearance in 1661. Up to that time the only postal markings on letters were handwritten, the purpose of such markings being to indicate the amount of postage paid or due. Only rarely were the dates of posting entered, except in the case of urgent letters on State business. These frequently had recorded upon them a complete timetable of arrivals and departures along the postal route, together with the time of ultimate delivery. Occasionally, on the front of the letter, they bore in conventional outline the drawing of a gallows as a warning to those who might be tempted to waylay the mail and sometimes they carried the inscription 'Haste, Post—Haste for Lyfe!'

Soon after the Restoration the Postmaster-General, Colonel Henry Bishop, stated in reply to charges of postal delays: 'A Stamp is invented, that is putt upon every letter shewing the day of the moneth that every letter comes to the office, so that no Letter Carryer may dare to detayne a letter from post to post, which before was usual.' In this way, with something of a flourish, the birth of the postmark was announced in England 'to prevent any neglect of the Letter Carryers in the speedy delivery of Letters'.

To Bishop, as Postmaster-General, was given credit for the 'invention' of postmarks but it is reasonably certain that he was not personally responsible for the innovation. He was a newcomer to postal work, having assumed office in 1660 as a 'farmer' or contractor at a rental of £21,500 a year for seven years. The original suggestion for the use of date-stamps probably derived from the promptings of experienced officials who had served under Cromwell's Commonwealth and, possibly, before under Charles I. Known to collectors today as 'Bishop Marks' (see figure 1), these pioneer date-stamps were used in London, Edinburgh, Dublin and in the British colonies of North America and India.

In other areas of the world—Australia and New Zealand, for example—the postal service, including the development of postmarks, has grown in more recent years. The first post office in Australia was opened at Sydney on 25 April 1809 in the home of the postmaster, Isaac Nichols, who also held other government appointments. This was for many years the only post office in New South Wales and it was not until 1 March 1828 that seven other post offices were established. These served Parramatta, Liverpool, Penrith, Bathurst, Windsor, Newcastle and Campbelltown. Between 1821 and 1841, when the first Australian suburban post office was opened at Ryde, the population of the colony had increased from just under 30,000 to almost 150,000. From this modest beginning the number of post offices in Australia had topped 7,700 by 1967.

New Zealand's postal history began with the opening, on the instructions of the Postmaster-General for New South Wales, of a small office in a general store in the Bay of Islands in 1831. With the arrival of Governor Hobson in 1840 the first post office of a more official nature was set up at Kororariki (now Russell) and the same year saw the establishment of offices in other settlements in the north and at Port Nicholson (Wellington). Eighteen years later—in 1858—73 post offices were functioning in New Zealand. By way of comparison, the number in operation in 1969 was 1,438.

From this necessarily superficial survey it can be seen that the scope for serious study of the cancellations of almost every region in the world is as wide as the student of postal history, or the individual collector, may wish to make it. Every region has its challenge and its special fascination. Geographical and political changes are constantly occurring and even the study of a minor region can be fruitful and enriching to the collector with an inquiring mind.

The gathering of very early material of postal history interest is exciting and rewarding, but no less than aspects of collecting cancellations which are, perhaps, even more within the scope and financial orbit of the general collector. With these varied opportunities in mind let us survey the world-wide field and assess some of the ways in which postal date-stamps old and new can offer pleasure to the researcher and the collector.

2
Surveying the field

If one wished at a given point in time to survey the world cancellations scene where and how could one begin? One might start by studying three fascinating volumes compiled and issued by the International Bureau of the Universal Postal Union in Berne, Switzerland. The first edition of *Dictionnaire des Bureaux de Poste* appeared in 1895. Subsequent editions followed in 1902, 1909, 1926, 1937, 1951 and (under the title *Nomenclature Internationale des Bureaux de Poste*) in 1968, and the stated aim of the UPU is to publish a new edition every five years.

The 1968 edition comprises a complete register of 437,168 principal post offices of UPU member-countries throughout the world, arranged in alphabetical sequence, with appropriate geographical sub-divisions—for example, name of state, province, county or postal district—in three volumes totalling 2,101 pages. Postal routing codes, where they exist, are also shown. An introductory 48-page booklet contains the preface and a broad outline of the plan and criteria observed in drawing up the three-volume list.

The first entry in Volume 1 is Aaback in the department of Vaasan lääni, Finland. The final entry, in Volume 3, is Zyznow in the province of Rzeszów in the Polish People's Republic. Between these two points are nearly half a million separate references to post offices in world states ranging alphabetically from Abu Dhabi in the Arabian Gulf to Zanzibar off the east coast of Africa.

A separately issued publication, *Statistique Complète des Services Postaux*, gives the statistical breakdown of the world's post offices under territorial headings, with details of the number of post offices and other statistical information for various member-countries of the UPU.

This, then, is an indication of the huge potential for the study of international postmarks.

As a broad means of post office identification these volumes are indispensable. More than that: they provide for the specialist in the cancellations of any particular country a virtually complete catalogue of recently issued items to be sought. The fortunate possessor of any of the pre-1939 editions could also, by comparing entries with the current edition, track the existence of post offices which formerly flourished and are now either obsolete or have changed their names. In the pages are listed—to quote two or three specimen regions—details of 3,034 post offices in South Africa, 40 in the Himalayan kingdom of Bhutan and 11,876 in Portugal. Here, also, are detailed 4,748 post offices in Finland, 44 in the Gaboon Republic, 5,165 in Mexico and 198 in Zambia. Bearing in mind the fact that these are simply sample listings, the collector can visualise what a wonderful field of world survey these books represent.

To the collector with an inquiring mind practically every name in the list is a challenge and an invitation. Hundreds of entertaining items leap to one's attention on even the most perfunctory examination: Jeddore Oyster Ponds, Nova Scotia; Andamooka Opal Fields, South Australia; Adekunle Bus Stop, Nigeria; Dynamite Factory, South Africa; Iwahig Penal Colony, Philippines, and so on. One need barely to have scratched the surface of toponymy to be attracted, intrigued and lured into exciting avenues of inquiry by such appealing place-names as Lazy Days, Baking Pot, Guinea Fowl, Solid Comfort, Gallon Jug and Joe Batt's Arm. What wonderlands of exploration, vicarious or personal, such place-names can invite!

Because the range is world-wide it is advisable at the outset to consider from which branch of the study one is likely to derive most satisfaction. Happily, there are no tailor-made limits. Even in this somewhat mercenary and materially-minded age there are pockets of activity where much material is still largely uncatalogued and uncommercialised. It remains, nevertheless, an advantage if the collector can visualise certain broad limits because the true objective of any collecting pastime is to tell a complete story, and no nebulous accumulation of oddments can achieve this.

First, the new collector must determine whether his material is to comprise old or modern specimens. How far back should he attempt to go? In Britain, for example, a convenient date by which to separate these two groups could be the turn of the present century. True, much fascinating material derives before that date, but if a demarcation line has to be named the dawn of a new century could be a convenient one. The year 1900 was also a heyday of the American scene. At that time 76,688 post offices were functioning in the United States (compared with 32,626 in 1967). Their histories and background stories reflect one of the most colourful expansionist phases in America's vivid history.

If we accept the desirability of taking a basic date—whether it be 1661, 1840, 1900 or whatever the individual collector's choice may be—we can pass to other matters which must be taken into account.

Of these the first is financial. Unless the collector is happily placed to obtain much material inexpensively, or unless he is exceptionally fortunate, the harvesting of pre-1900 postal markings may prove to be a costly process. Early material of postal history interest has acquired considerable rarity value in recent years and fetches high prices in auctions as we shall see in the chapter on postal history values.

Conversely, a creditable collection of early postal matter can be built up quite inexpensively if the enthusiast can enlist diligence and patience as his allies in the search. Personal search and inquiry can produce much suitable material from one's own sources of contact and membership of an appropriate society or club can enlarge the scope for exchange and purchase of likely items. Many philatelic dealers stock and sell postal history material and, especially in provincial centres, early postmarks and covers can often be acquired at relatively low cost.

In general, however, the building of a pre-1900 collection in many world areas could be prohibitively expensive for the average collector, whereas a post-1900 collection could be developed without any serious drain on the resources and would be no less interesting on that account.

Whatever the chronological limits, another fundamental decision would be to determine the geographical boundaries of one's collecting interest. Here the scope is so wide, and yet so conveniently adjustable, that hardly any problem arises. Many collectors have limited their activities and their research to the specific town, county, state or country in which they live or on which their special interest centres.

Many really admirable studies have been undertaken, for example, within such relatively narrow geographical limits as Aden, Jamaica, Fiji, the Antarctic, Christmas Island, the Borough of Huddersfield (England), the Yukon Territory or the state of New South Wales, Australia.

The specific regional study offers, perhaps, the richest rewards. Almost anyone can become an authority on the postal history of his, or her, own home town or county. Research facilities and opportunities may differ, but they are invariably more promising in one's own locality and as a general rule encouragement is given to the collector anxious to put on record aspects of local history.

Admirable guidance has from time to time been given in philatelic publications on how to compile a local postal history collection. One such article by George F. Crabb, a committee member of the British Postmark Society, was published in the society's quarterly bulletin in January 1970. Taking the municipal borough of Epsom (Surrey, England) as the basis of his study, Mr Crabb showed how a local study with regionally limited objectives could be made to reflect not only the postal history but also something of the social history and life of a particular community. A wealth of literature is now available in the form of monographs, handbooks and full-length illustrated works covering the postal history and cancellations of many widely scattered world areas.

Let us examine two contrasting examples in this field and note how individual researchers tackled areas of interest dictated by their own collecting preferences and opportunities.

In October 1968, Eric Buckley, of Sheffield, England, a Fellow of the Society of Postal Historians, published a 70-page monograph on *The Postal History of Huddersfield*. This West Riding town is an important and thriving borough in the North of England, a place like many others of similar calibre steeped in regional history but limited—one might have thought—in opportunities for the development of a worthwhile study of postal history. The error of such an assumption was made clear by Mr Buckley in the course of a fascinating and patient study.

He began by outlining the town's general history and then developed, through the centuries, the story of its routes of communication. Here is a typical sidelight from the situation at the turn of the nineteenth century, culled from a local newspaper report:

In the early 1800s the postal service of this town was an entirely female affair. At the Head Post Office in Old Street (now Kirkgate) the presiding spirit was a woman of character known throughout the district as 'Old Mrs Murgatroyd'. She did everything. There is more than a hint that she was a formidable figure, but she was obviously better educated than most working women of her day. It was her job to mark the price on each letter as it was handed in and the charges were somewhat involved, varying sharply not only with weight, but with distance. Her sole assistant was an ageing lady, Mrs Brooksbank, the postwoman. Not that she called herself anything so ordinary. In the best traditions of Civil Service English she was known as the Female Letter Carrier.

Mr Buckley develops the story and illustrates, as far as possible, each phase of the town's postal history with handstamps and, in later pages, machine cancellations. Highlights of local history are produced and recorded as part of the postal scene. We learn that tram car mail operated in the town in the 1890s and details are given of the types of handstamps and machine cancellers used over several centuries of the town's history. The study is rounded off with a chronological list of postmasters and head postmasters and a list of letter-receiving offices established in the town from the earliest times.

By way of sharp contrast an area very different from England's industrial north was the study focus of H. M. Campbell, FRPSL, who in 1957 published a monograph dealing with the post offices and postal cancellations of Fiji. After outlining the islands' early postal history, beginning with the carriage of mail in the schooner *Blackbird* in 1835, he traced the history of postal date-stamps used in many of the principal communities, with appropriate illustrations of many of the types.

One section of Mr Campbell's study included a detailed list, in alphabetical order, of Fijian post offices with details of the types of cancellations used, and the monograph ended with a survey of Service cancellations used in the islands during the Second World War.

According to one's nature and inclinations, one may pioneer a new field or add to the published knowledge of an existing one. Or one may collect material purely from personal interest, for private pleasure, extending the frontiers of one's own knowledge.

For the collector in this field there are no rigid rules. The limpid heat of equatorial seaports or the chill silence of Alaskan settlements can be evoked by acquisition of postal date-stamps from Mombasa, Shungnak, Dar-es-Salaam or Ketchikan. With its postmark to spotlight one's interest on the place one may piece together the remarkable story of Medicine Hat, Alberta, or gather in postmark form the communications history of Montana, Bangladesh, Burundi, Montserrat or Malaysia.

Whatever one's choice, old or new, parochial or world wide, the joy of the search is likely to remain constant. How, then, does one begin to acquire material; what sources of supply can one tap? With these two questions it might now be appropriate to concern ourselves.

3
Sources of supply

After the first year or two most collectors of cancellations and covers find that the problem is not how to tap and encourage sources of supply, but how to accommodate and arrange the cascading inflow of material.

Initially, the flow can be stimulated in many different ways—the first of which is to contact other collectors and make known one's interests and needs. Almost every collector has an immediate circle of friends, fellow enthusiasts and business or social contacts. It is from these sources that the nucleus of a collection can be started.

Although the collector must first define his own interests and line of approach, a generally sound principle is to accept all material in the early stages of forming a collection, bearing in mind that what is irrelevant for one's own purposes may be admirable for another's. It will be found, also, that a pre-requisite of satisfactory exchange with other enthusiasts is to have available a wide and versatile range of negotiable items.

Some general advice may suggest a few of the many ways in which material can be obtained and it is often the case that once such a start has been made one's fellow enthusiasts are only too glad to help.

For the collector of pre-1840 material the field is largely restricted to specimens obtainable through dealers who specialise in postal history items, bidding at postal history auctions or buying from dealers at philatelic exhibitions, exchanging with members of a collectors' club or through various commercial or private channels.

There is a growing number of dealers and firms specialising in specific categories of material, such as those connected with aero-philately, special event hand-stamps, first day covers, and postal history material. The advertisement columns of the world's philatelic press will suggest many outlets of this type through which the foundations of a collection can be laid.

Occasionally, that varying fortune which enables philatelists and connoisseurs of antiques to acquire items of great value for trifling sums will similarly smile on the cancellations collector. Old letters bearing interesting postmarks have, for instance, been discovered between the leaves of books where they have lain forgotten for years. Librarians often discover and discard old collections of local correspondence. General dealers who buy household bric-à-brac are another surprisingly fruitful source from which old correspondence bearing rare imprints can occasionally come to light. The lumber rooms of country houses and rural cottages and the archives of legal offices and old-established commercial concerns are further sources for the discovery of hoarded documents—and since these are often worthless to their possessors they can often be obtained quite reasonably at small cost.

From these sources and from the generosity of friends and fellow collectors the student of postal history may hope to gather material with which to begin and later develop his collection. Once a start has been made it is astonishing how quickly and from what varied sources new acquisitions begin to arrive.

For the collector of modern material the opportunities for gathering specimens are greatly increased and prevailing prices are usually less formidable.

Here are a few suggestions for obtaining material in this category:

1 Personal approach to post offices, using self-addressed envelopes, or by any one of several other legitimate means of obtaining date-stamp impressions. These include impressions given on forms of receipt for the purchase of postage and insurance stamps, receipts given for registered letters and (in the United Kingdom) for recorded mail, and certificates of posting issued for parcels and letter post items.

2 Overseas postmasters will often respond to requests for post-

marks when these are accompanied by appropriate return postage or reply coupons.

3 Judicious purchase of kiloware and missionary packets often provide good selections of postal markings.

4 Millions of unwanted postmarks are dumped daily by commercial and industrial firms and by nationalised bodies. It is often possible to arrange for the periodical collection of such material.

5 Personal contacts at home and overseas will often gather material on one's behalf, perhaps on an exchange or payment basis.

6 Private arrangements can sometimes be made with large mail order firms to take over accumulations of unwanted used envelopes.

Another rich store-room in which postmarks abound are the albums of picture postcards amassed by collectors in the late nineteenth and early twentieth centuries. During the past 80 years or so thousands of picture postcards have been issued and literally millions of them have passed through the world's postal channels. For many people the urge to collect these has been reawakened in recent years by some fine studies of the subject, but in attics and store-rooms of hundreds of homes there still lie dusty albums between whose covers are postcards bearings first class postal imprints of bygone years.

It should not be assumed that cancellation collecting is a strictly indoor pastime. Walking tours, coach and car journeys and air-flights make it possible to compile on-the-spot notes which will greatly enrich the collection when it comes to be written up.

Esperantists and friends with wide overseas business connections can be of great assistance. The former, unhampered by linguistic barriers, are often prolific correspondents on a worldwide scale; the latter often have access to a collector's treasure house of discarded items of mail from every corner of the globe. There are also philatelic merchandising services which, for varying fees, will obtain and despatch direct to the subscriber covers bearing special handstamps and slogans.

To assist collectors directly, the British Post Office introduced in June 1971 a printed *Postmark Bulletin* giving advance details of postmark slogans and special handstamps available through official channels. There is, indeed, a widespread tendency in many post office administrations throughout the world to establish a good relationship with cover and hand-stamp collectors and postal historians. The Australian Post Office, for example, issues an admirable bulletin with notes, news and illustrations about forth-coming postmarks; the case histories of specific Australian post offices are researched, published and distributed by the Director of Posts and Telegraphs at Sydney, Australia. In Canada *The Post-mark*, published monthly at Ottawa, serves the interests of the Canadian postal service and includes many notes of relevance to collectors. Other postal administrations are equally helpful.

Finally, but by no means least in importance, membership of one or more of a growing number of societies and study circles catering for various branches of this collecting hobby could be quoted as an admirable means of enriching the collection and the knowledge of the enthusiast who is sufficiently interested to apply for membership.

Details of some of these organisations—they are world-wide and numerous—are given in chapter 15. They include the Post-mark Club (UK, founded 1883); the British Postmark Society (UK, founded 1958); the Postal History Society (UK, founded 1936); the Postal History Society, Inc., (USA), the Postmark Collectors' Club (USA, founded 1946); the South African Postmark Society (founded 1969) and the Postal History Society of New Zealand (founded 1964).

Some of these societies provide exchange facilities by means of circulating packets or the postal auction of members' material. Others sponsor and publish authoritative handbooks, monographs and bulletins on various aspects of postal history, postal cancellations and associated subjects.

4
Housing and Writing up the Collection

Part of the attraction of postmark collecting is that there are few predetermined rules and from the earliest times its devotees have pursued individual lines of research and inquiry.

For that reason one hesitates to suggest methods of housing a collection of postmarks and allied material, yet there remain some basic principles and hints on methods which the beginner and the advanced collector alike may find useful.

It is as well at the outset to try to determine some objectives: What is the aim of the collection?

What are the foreseeable limits of its scope?

Is the collection to be concentrated on modern material? If not, how far back into postal history does one intend to probe?

Does the collector intend to gather covers or cut-outs (postmarks on piece) or both?

Is the aim to develop a thematic collection, a regional collection or one based on historical, geographical or chronological limits?

What space is foreseeably available for accommodating the collection?

How much time and money does one intend to expend upon it?

These are a few of the fundamental points one might consider. A little thought before one sets out to adopt a particular method of housing and arranging one's material is well worthwhile and may avoid the need for drastic, frustrating and expensive revision at some later stage.

Whichever system one adopts, it should be flexible and allow for expansion. It should be capable of absorbing fluctuations in the availability of material and of accommodating changes in postal procedures and those brought about by territorial and political alterations.

Here are some further points to which the collector might give consideration:

Give your material the dignity of space; do not cramp the units by placing them too close together.

Allow ample space for writing up the specimens in an informative and entertaining way.

Use scissors only with care, remembering that a cut, once made, can never be unmade.

Never remove the adhesive stamps or postal markings from a cover likely to be of historical, philatelic or general interest. The value is much greater if the whole envelope remains intact. A bundle of letters, for example, mailed from India or Australia 50 or 100 years ago may show the postal rates, routes taken, time in transit and many other points of interest. Even if the letters are not associated with any notable person or event they may be of great sociological interest and be of immense research value to later generations.

Wherever possible display the postmark and the adhesive stamp together. Combined in this way, the story they tell may have greater impact and may be given in much greater detail.

Remember that a collection of postmarks is not a collection of adhesive stamps and equally a collection of adhesive stamps is not a collection of postmarks. The two things are quite different and the aim of the collector should be to acquire material for the specific type of collection he has in mind.

Reject imperfect specimens—for example, postal markings which are hopelessly smudged or dirty or below reasonable limits of acceptability.

Be prepared to discover all you can about the history, background, places of origin, mailing methods and personalities connected with the postal markings in your collection. Bear in mind the possibility of studying the social and commercial development and the political history of the area on which you are concentrating so that your collection will portray the part played by the postal service in the social life of the community.

Remember the Maine

1898   1933

Commemorating the
35TH ANNIVERSARY OF THE
SINKING OF
U. S. S. MAINE
IN HAVANA HARBOR
February 15, 1898

EDWARD HACKER
P. O. Box 11
Hammond, Indiana

GREETINGS FROM
SAVOONGA, ALASKA

Most Western Postoffice
on the American Continent.

Sponsored by
REV. T. A. MOYER, Ludington, Michigan.

I Special covers, USA

At this point a few words on my own method of accommodating material may be of interest, but it should be borne in mind that my system is designed to serve my own special purposes as a collector-journalist and may not appeal to collectors in other specialised areas of activity.

Primarily, my aim is to acquire at least one good, clear strike from as many different post offices as possible throughout the world, especially those sited in remote places or those with entertaining background stories. It follows that I prefer to acquire not only the postmark but also authentic notes about the place from which it derived. The method by which I classify and file my material is on simple, direct lines.

One section is devoted entirely to covers. These are placed in re-sealable transparent polythene envelopes, size $8\frac{1}{2}$ inches by 5 inches (216 mm by 127 mm). Each envelope is numbered in the top left-hand corner by means of a small, white self-adhesive seal. The envelopes are housed in filing cabinets with drawers. A corresponding record card, size $5\frac{1}{2}$ inches by $3\frac{1}{2}$ inches (140 mm by 89 mm) contains the geographical name and location of each item and the identification number of the polythene envelope in which it can be found.

These covers section record cards are housed within the main body of the collection which consists of some 150,000 cut-out postmarks, on piece, filed alphabetically in country order on $5\frac{1}{2}$ inch by $3\frac{1}{2}$ inch (140 mm by 89 mm) record cards.

The postmark cut-outs are stamp-hinged on to these cards, on the reverse side of which are given any notes of relevant interest regarding the background, postal history or geographical location of the postmark's place of origin. If I wish to show variations in the different types of handstamps and machine cancellations or postal slogans used in any particular place additional cards are made out.

A smaller, specialised part of my personal collection—also accommodated in polythene self-seal transparent envelopes—comprises the historical section. Its purpose is to trace the chronological development of the postmark and the arrangement is strictly in date-of-use sequence.

The record cards, which serve as an index to the whole collection, are housed in filing cabinets with double-compartment

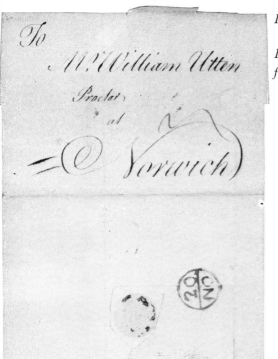

I Types of early Bishop Marks

II Back and front of original letter from Lady Mary Roche, 1798

drawers, each cabinet accommodating about 25,000 cards.

This method suits my purpose splendidly, and enables me to cope with changes and expansion in any section. Place-name and territorial changes are easily dealt with by cross-references or by making out new cards for newly-established territories.

If this method is not suitable, there are any number of alternatives which can be considered.

Albums and binders for covers are now readily available in a wide range of sizes, prices and types which may suit the needs of some collectors. Another effective type of accommodation can be devised by adapting one's own form of loose-leaf album, using photographic corner mounts, or by purchasing one of the many types on sale through dealers. The 'ring' type of binder may be particularly suitable for some purposes. These are available in a variety of shapes and sizes and the type selected should have leaves of good quality to withstand constant handling.

A refinement of the loose-leaf method is to use the larger type of photograph album, say 10 inches by 8 inches (254 mm by 203 mm), with black loose-leaf refill sheets, using white ink for any notes which may be necessary. The dark background greatly enhances the appearance of the postmarks or covers and if the material is neatly spaced it can be very effective.

Other useful accessories which may be mentioned briefly include a 4 inch by 2 inch (100 mm by 50 mm) templet, or guide, to ensure uniformity in the size of postmark cut-outs; spade-ended tweezers for picking up individual postmarks, a high-power glass magnifier (preferably mounted) and a gauge for measuring the diameter of postmarks.

Pre-gummed mounts, with a black background can also be purchased, and gummed title strips showing countries may be a useful accessory for some collectors.

It is easily possible to combine with postmark collecting the skill and pleasure of photography by taking photographs—having obtained appropriate permission—of offices whose postmarks are represented in one's collection. Photographs may also be taken of county boundary signs which can serve as an interesting page or section title for a regional collection or display.

An entirely different method of display, suitable for exhibitions or as a visual aid for a school room can be achieved by mounting the map of a country, county, provice or other geographical division upon some suitable dark-surfaced material of paper or board. The background material should be larger than the map, providing a dark margin in which to display a variety of postal date-stamps from towns and villages and centres of interest in the area covered by the map. A leader-tape may then be run from the postmark in the margin to the point on the map from which it derived.

To assist in identifying postmarks whose source of origin is obscure and of general help in writing up the collection there are many aids. Guide books, maps and gazetteers are an obvious channel for the discovery of background facts about out-of-the-way places; in addition there are many invaluable official publicacations. Typifying the best of these is the *Dictionnaire des Bureaux de Poste* to which reference has been made in chapter 2. At the level of individual countries and regions separate directories are usually available.

In Britain the appropriate 500-page publication to date is entitled *Post Offices in the United Kingdom*. A modestly-priced publication, it contains the postal and telegraphic address of every post office in Great Britain (except London, for which a separate edition is available) including Northern Ireland, the Channel Islands, the Isle of Man and the Republic of Ireland.

In the United States of America a comparable publication is the *Directory of Post Offices*, an annual publication revised as at 1 July each year. It is the official list of post offices, named stations, branches and rural stations, with many items of information relating to each. A preliminary summary gives details of American post offices, by classes, in each state and territory.

In Canada information about post offices and their locations is given in *List of Post Offices in Canada*, published in English and French; in Australia, East Africa and the Republic of Ireland it is listed in the official *Post Office Guide*; in South Africa a biannual edition of *Post Offices in the Republic of South Africa* provides similar details and in virtually every member-country of the Universal Postal Union comparable information is available.

As well as these sources, supporting services of many kinds provide an admirable flow of helpful material. For example, in the United States of America the General Services Department of the National Archives and Records Services at Washington, DC, can co-operate with the provision of information about post offices dating from pre-1929. For post-1929 information about American post offices the appropriate source is the Post Office Department of the Bureau of Operations, Postmasters and Rural Appointments Division, also at Washington, DC.

In Great Britain much valuable information is housed in the Bruce Castle Museum (Tottenham, London N17), the National Postal Museum, the British Museum and the National Maritime Museum, all sited in London.

The resources of the British Post Office Record Room are also of great value to collectors who wish to pursue aspects of local postal history. An extensive philatelic and postal history collection is accommodated in the Midlands city of Birmingham and, further north, in the Philatelic Section of the Central Reference Library, Leeds.

Here, in summary, is a guide to some of the facilities available at the British Post Office Record Room as outlined in a guide distributed by the British Post Office:

In conjunction with a study of State Papers (Domestic) published by the Public Record Office a postal study of a town can commence from 1543. Indexed volumes are available which include transcriptions of letters concerning the management of the King's posts (i.e. before 1635) and the subsequent State postal service.

The earliest original records in the Record Room cover the period 1672–1677 and give a comprehensive picture of the postal services of their day. From 1677 until the early 1790s the information is more limited although it includes the names and salaries of postmasters and the site of post towns of the period. In 1790 an important series of records on matters affecting the Post Office came into being, supported by letters and reports from local postmasters and residents, and continued in this form until 1836. Also of great interest to the local historian in this field is a series of coloured postal maps, dating from 1807, which depict foot, horse and mail coach routes and the various local penny post networks operating at that time.

From independent sources such as the Commonwealth Institute, London, helpful material including Commonwealth fact sheets can be obtained, and from the Director of Posts and Telegraphs in Sydney, Australia, well-documented histories of individual Australian post offices are issued.

Taking these as a basis, it can be said that the postal authorities of most overseas countries are extremely helpful to the genuine collector and researcher. Many countries in common with Great Britain, America, Canada, Australia and New Zealand maintain efficient post office public relations departments from which an inquiry accompanied by an appropriate International Reply Coupon will invariably elicit the information required. Moreover, reprint techniques used for the re-issuing of old directories, and photo-copying facilities, are now so sophisticated that records and details once unobtainable to the distant researcher are now readily available.

With these background sources in mind, how should one set about the exercise of writing up a postmark collection in an instructive and pleasing manner?

On this subject all sorts of advice could be given, much of it conflicting and arguable. Opinions will vary. But the present writer's personal advice is to approach the exercise *as if one were writing a non-fiction book*. If one tackles the writing-up of a thematic or a general collection of postmark material in this way one begins at the outset to establish clear lines of method and intention.

This plan will have other advantages. It will tend to keep one's material strictly relevant; it will help to discipline the collector into making his material of interest not only to himself but to a much wider public; it will assist him to present his material in an orderly way; it will establish clear guide-lines and encourage him to place the maximum emphasis on accuracy, honesty and objectivity. Books are written to instruct, entertain, amuse or to inform the reader: to impart knowledge and to stimulate thought. Above all, they must never be dull.

What ingredients might one expect a well-written, non-fiction book to possess?

One would expect it to be accurate and to have something to say; to have shape and continuity; perhaps to be well-illustrated;

2   Same name links

to entertain, instruct or inform and, perhaps, to quote dependable sources from which further information could be obtained if desired. It should also be well-produced, aesthetically pleasing in appearance and possess a well-defined literary shape which fulfilled its purpose within the limitations of its stated scope and object.

All these elements are almost exactly what a sensibly compiled collection of postmarks and postal history material should possess.

First, select a title and theme reflecting your own collecting preference. Then select, arrange and present your material in logical conformity with the title you have chosen. Keep the writing-up of your material as light and lively as possible. Even scholarly research can be presented in a readable and entertaining way.

Avoid writing about your collection as if you were compiling a catalogue. Try to infuse enthusiasm, colour and interest into your subject—because this is what a study of postmarks is all about. For example, here are some background notes compiled by the Australian Postmaster General's Department concerning certain novel features of mail delivery:

One of the characteristic features of Australian mail runs is the distance traversed and the loneliness of the mailman on his long and tiring journeys. Operating from the far west of New South Wales, for instance, there is one service which covers a distance of 728 miles (1,172 km) and extends into three States. It is the service from Tibooburra to Cordillo Downs and it is carried out once a fortnight . . .

On the journey the mailman travels 36 miles (58 km) in New South Wales, crosses the Queensland border at Warri Gate and then travels 165 miles (265 km) in Queensland before he crosses the South Australian border to go to Innamincka which is about 20 miles (32 km) further on . . .

In the vast, sparsely-populated northern district of Western Australia where the terrain is particularly difficult the road mail service is one of the most important means of communication.

The Meekatharra-Marble Bar Service, which covers a distance of 1,164 miles (1,874 km) is one of the loneliest and most hazardous in the British Commonwealth. Numerous water courses, river beds and marshes, which become raging torrents or quagmires after heavy rain, tax the resources of the mailman but he usually manages to make the difficult crossings with the minimum of delay.

With a view to keeping residents along the route informed of the movements of the mail vehicle, arrangements have been made with the Australian Broadcasting Commission for progress reports to be broadcast over National stations...

Supporting material in the form of postal slogans, covers, photographs, diagrams, sketches and press clippings may have a part to play in the building of one's collection. To these may be added relevant correspondence and personal notes—'atmosphere material'—which help to convey more intimately than any amount of dust-dry data the background story of the people and places and the community life to which one's postmark material is related.

5
Postmarks, Places and People

There is in Europe, according to some viewpoints, an almost wilful tradition that postmark studies and allied research into areas of postal history should be presented in a somewhat solid, heavy manner which could seem dull to anyone save the most dedicated and devoted specialist reader. This criticism—with which the present writer does not wholly agree—is levelled less frequently against comparable works published in America and the British Commonwealth countries.

It must, however, be admitted that many otherwise admirable monographs and handbooks tend somewhat to justify the term 'dull'. Although they bear the hallmark of scholarly research, and obviously represent the fruits of dedicated and enthusiastic personal involvement and are of genuine interest to collectors in the specialised fields with which they deal, they are sometimes so concerned with finite detail that it could be said they lack colour and human interest.

As one writer expressed it, in another context, 'No hypnotism takes place, luring one on to a study of page after page . . .' Instead, the reader—like Lewis Carroll's Alice—is tempted to ponder 'What is the use of a book without pictures and conversations?'; or, to paraphrase the same source, he may say to himself 'This book tells me far more than I wish to know about (for example) the postmarks of Poland, Pakistan or Peru.'

Despite these criticisms, an apparently insignificant detail of a postal cancellation can uncover entrancing areas of investigation. When a Queensland specialist wishes to acquire early-use speci-

mens of the State's postage stamps, a criteria which might mat-
erially assist him is specific knowledge of the type of obliterator
used in Queensland before its separation from New South Wales.
Similarly, a B62 cancellation on a Hong Kong adhesive is signif-
icantly different in value and meaning from the rare 62B cancellation from the same source, and a 6M postmark of Managua,
Nicaragua if offered on a complete cover would certainly not be
insignificant to a philatelic auctioneer. How, also, could one hope
to identify a VOC 6 ST handstamp—the first postmark used at the
Cape of Good Hope—without the help of a close-focus study of
the various types in use at that time in that region?

Minute shades of detail are, therefore, of very real importance
to the collector, not only because they lead to an understanding of
postmark values but as an aid to the fullest appreciation of the
hobby. Perhaps the omission—this apparent unwillingness to
breathe life into the study—is due to a failure to see the subject in
its three dimensional aspects?

Several years ago Kathleen Partridge, a British writer and poet,
wrote:

> *The postmark on a letter always means*
> *so much to me;*
> *It is a tiny circle into which I seem to see*
> *A place, a time, a person, a purpose and*
> *a thought,*
> *Plus the intervening towns through which*
> *the letter has been brought.*

This viewpoint, sentimental and over-simplified though it may
be, is somewhere near the heart of the matter. When we begin to
see, instead of a mere humble black imprint upon the face of a
letter, a symbolic link with distant lands and different modes of
life we may be beginning, at last, to infuse life into our subject.

There is, if one chooses to look for it, a story behind many
seemingly commonplace postmarks. The story may be that of the
issuing office, or of some curious local usage; it may be a scrap of
local lore or a matter of historical or sociological fact. It may be
connected with a man or woman after whom the place was named;
it may be a peculiarity of the postmark itself, a fragment of a

community's life or even a link with the history of our time.

There is a postmark from Sydney, Australia which bears the date 19 March 1932 and the slogan 'Posted on Bridge During Opening Celebrations'. There is one from Longyearbyen, Spitzbergen—a mining settlement on the Arctic fringe—where the post office opened only when a vessel could be seen cautiously nudging its way up Advent Fjord. Another postmark with a romantic story is that of the Golden Temple, Amritsar, India. The temple, created at fabulous cost from material which included marble, copper and gold leaf, was built primarily to house Granth Sahib, the sacred book of the Sikhs.

Let us take in outline the background stories of some of the postmarks featured in the illustration pages of this book.

One of these places is Golf, which reportedly consisted—at the time of the compilation of the writer's own notes regarding the place—of a community of 120 houses and 400 people in Cook County, Illinois, USA. The township and its post office came into existence in the 1920s when a railroad tycoon required facilities for playing golf at the Glen View Golf and Polo Club. He used to have the Chicago-Milwaukee train stopped in open country near the clubhouse—presumably a somewhat inconvenient arrangement which he decided to simplify. Thus, a special siding was built to accommodate the rail car. Later, houses were built in the vicinity and a community began to develop under the name Golf Village, which was eventually shortened, in postmark form, to Golf.

On the face of it, the postmark of Miller's Dale, Derbyshire, England, is a mediocre and unremarkable exhibit, yet it has an interesting affinity with that of Golf. For years Miller's Dale post office, 6 miles (9 km) east of Bakewell, was established on a mainline railway station platform, one of few such offices in England. In charge of the office until it closed on 4 March 1967 was subpostmaster Harry Hartshorn who combined with his postal duties those of a railway station booking clerk.

A survey of the background sources of postal markings soon reveals the extraordinary variety of premises and buildings in which post offices may be sited.

The mail office at Wellington Hospital, New Zealand, was (and may still be) located along a polished corridor opposite Ward 2 (see figure XII). At Paremoremo, also in New Zealand, the local post office, opened in November 1960, was housed in a settlement planned to accommodate prison staff and their families. Butterley post office, near Derby, England, was, in 1966, sited in a tiny octagonal building which had the appearance of a Martello tower from the anxious days of the Napoleonic wars.

At Coober Pedy, in the opal fields of central South Australia, the post office was at one time in its history located underground, down what used to be an old mine shaft, in an attempt to escape from the blistering heat and sun-glare. An *Adelaide Advertiser* interviewer in 1947 described Bill Oliver, then Coober Pedy's postmaster, as 'one of the well-known characters of the opal fields who had come to the place with his lungs full of gas after the 1914–18 War and had been there ever since.' Bill Oliver's post office was an underground dug-out with electric light supplied by a small generator. The accommodation comprised a small kitchen, a bed-sitting room and a workroom fitted with a forge. Appropriately, Coober Pedy's name, derived from an aboriginal source, means 'hole in the ground'.

By way of contrast, the post office at Gore, Ohio, USA, was in 1968 installed in a sparkling green-and-white mobile home and at Braunston, in the pocket-sized county of Rutland, England, it is sited in graceful premises erected as a Methodist chapel in 1868.

At the North Pole post office, 14 miles (23 km) east of Fairbanks, Alaska, the postmaster transacts business in an extraordinary igloo-shaped edifice. Across the Atlantic at Ribe, Denmark, similar services are provided in historic premises called the Taarnborg, dating from 1550; and outgoing mail from one post office at Rizal in the Philippines is franked 'New Bilibid Prison'.

A dot on the map north of Calgary denotes the site of Dog Pound, Alberta, Canada. But the map does not tell Dog Pound's story. It leaves one to guess whether the place is a corral for delinquent dogs or whether people actually live there and its name stems from some other derivation. In fact, when a post office was opened in 1894, 4 miles (6 km) from the present village, it bore the name Bradbourne. This was a tribute to a village in Derbyshire, England, which had been the postmaster's birthplace.

It has been said that there was once another Bradbourne in

Manitoba (it no longer appears on the map) and on this account, to avoid confusion, the Alberta village changed its name to Dog Pound in 1905.

The name is probably of Indian origin, derived either from Dogpound, an Indian chief who lived in the district in 1883, or from a translation of the Cree name for the sound of dogs pounding along the nearby creek as the braves returned from their winter camp. The railroad reached Dog Pound about 1930. Thirty-five years later the village consisted of a grain elevator, a post office store, a bulk gas and oil business and four houses in which lived the 17 inhabitants whose main occupation was farming.

Yellow Jacket—an American colloquialism for what in other English-speaking countries might be called a hornet or wasp—is listed in the 1967 US Directory as a fourth-class post office in Montezuma County, Colorado.

Why this curious name?

The explanation seems to be that the early map-makers gave to a canyon in this region its strange, descriptive title because the walls of the canyon were plastered with yellow jacket nests. An equally feasible suggestion is that the settlement which developed near the canyon was named for Old Chief Yellow Jacket—'a mean old skunk' according to one chronicler—who was chief of the Navajo Indians. A post office was opened here in 1914 and named for the canyon. But in 1943 the *Colorado Magazine* recorded that Yellow Jacket's population totalled only seven persons, so its survival in postmark form may well be in jeopardy.

Misery is not an attractive name but it exists on the map and as a postmark. It is a village in Fribourg canton, Switzerland, on the Berne-Lausanne line and in 1960 its population was 241.

On similar lines is Silly, a self-respecting village of about 1,500 inhabitants 7 miles (11 km) east of Ath in a chicory-growing region of Hainaut province, Belgium. The Flemish form of the name is Opzullik but if one posts a letter in the village it will be given a Silly postmark. Of course, in its place-name context Misery does not imply distress, wretchedness, woe or tribulation, nor does Belgium's Silly look quaint to Belgians. But occasionally such names raise a smile even in their own country of origin. (See figure 3.)

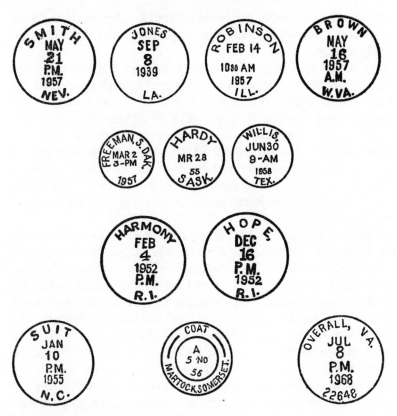

3 *Apt associations*

Bradford, England, has a suburban post office called Idle (a local society runs an Idle Youth Centre) and in Italy there are postal centres respectively named Cipollina ('Little Onion') and Budino ('Pudding'). Another worthwhile acquisition is the postmark of La Porcherie, France. The village lies in the department of Haute Vienne and for centuries its inhabitants have had to put up with jokes about the name, which translates as 'The Piggery'.

The postmark of Salvation, Natal, South Africa, has an interesting background story. The post office there is sited on a settlement and farm run by the Salvation Army. To get to it one has to travel about 50 miles (80 km) along the Vryheid-Nongoma road and mail goes out and comes in by an African runner three times

45

a week. The post office serves 88 African kraals and their people as well as a 65-bed Bantu hospital, a farm school and divisional headquarters.

By what tantalising trick of destiny does the surname of a modest, gentle Englishwoman who spent the first 35 years of her life in the sheltered repose of a Cornish parsonage come to be imprinted on the map of South Africa? Hobhouse is the name. This village, a community of 1000 people, founded in 1904, lies about 75 miles (120 km) east of Bloemfontein, in the Orange Free State, near the Lesotho border. Many of its farms, originally allocated to British ex-servicemen who fought in the Boer War, still bear such Britannic names as Essex, England, New Scotland and Langley Park.

Emily Hobhouse, social worker, reformer and humanitarian is the woman in whose honour the village is named. Born on 9 April 1860, the fifth living child of Reginald Hobhouse, Rector of St Ive, Cornwall, England, she took up welfare work in America after her father's death in 1895. Then came the South African War. Moved by stories of hardship among the Boer women and children, she visited South Africa and worked unceasingly to improve conditions for those who were, in name at least, her country's enemies. To the Boer women Emily Hobhouse was 'The Angel of Love'. But although she was a member of an influential political family she had to overcome serious opposition, including arrest and deportation, in her efforts to focus attention on conditions in South Africa.

Miss Hobhouse died in 1926. Accorded a State funeral at which a moving oration was spoken by General Smuts, she was buried at the foot of the South African National Monument, near Bloemfontein. Her name, though revived by the publication of a biography in 1972, is sometimes in danger of being forgotten except in the little South African village which bears it.

Typifying the kind of confusion that can sometimes arise because of an unusual place-name is the story of J. Michelson, a South African businessman who in 1957 was on his way in a station wagon to a philatelic congress in Paarl. At first all went well. Then suddenly, in a desolate spot 30 miles (48 km) from Beaufort West, the station wagon broke down and Mr Michelson found himself stranded. Happily help came . . . but Mr Michelson's station wagon, consigned in its unrunnable condition by rail to Johannesburg, unaccountably turned up at a far distant point of what was then called Southern Rhodesia. Apparently in an attempt to obtain carriage for the damaged vehicle at a special rate, the repair garage had marked its consignment papers with the word 'Concession'—unaware that this was also the name of a railway station and post office about 40 miles (64 km) north of Salisbury. The difficulties involved in recovering the vehicle were almost unending. The car had twice crossed the border. Both an import and export permit were demanded and only negotiations at the highest level over a long period of time enabled Mr Michelson eventually to regain possession of his station wagon.

The township whose name caused all the trouble has a population of about 450 and stands 450 feet (140 m) above sea-level north of Salisbury. Its name stems from the fact that a concession was granted by the British South Africa Company to Moore's Rhodesia Concession in this area in October 1895.

Cadell, South Australia, is another postmark whose background invites more than cursory research. Its village of origin lies in an irrigation area on the left bank of the Murray river, about 4 miles (6 km) east of Morgan and 90 miles (144 km) north-east of Adelaide. Francis Cadell, whose name this postmark recalls, was born at the East Lothian fishing village of Cockenzie, Scotland, in February 1822. Educated in Edinburgh and Germany, he chose a sea-faring career and after numerous adventures arrived in Australia in 1849. One of his most famous exploits was when he entered a government sponsored race for the first steamer to navigate the Murray river. He had the steamer *Lady Augusta* specially built and in her explored the river system. For these services he received a gold candelabrum worth 900 guineas (£945) and a gold medal was struck in his honour.

This was one event in an adventure-filled life which included service in the Chinese War, pearl fishing, whaling and exploration and pioneer navigation in Australia and New Zealand. He died in mysterious circumstances near Ambiona in the Dutch East Indies in 1879 and most authorities agree that his services as a pioneer navigator were never fully appreciated during his lifetime. For such a man perhaps a place on the map comes as fitting, if belated, recognition.

The postmark of Cinema, British Columbia, Canada, pinpoints another fascinating area of research. Although no longer listed by the Universal Postal Union, a post office—originally named Cinema City—existed here in 1957. Its name was a quaint throwback to the pioneer days of the celluloid screen: a link with the era of Valentino, Charlie Chaplin, Chester Conklin and the Keystone Cops. Describing the hamlet in a letter dated 7 September 1957 Postmaster H. Bryant wrote: 'Cinema lies in the famous Cariboo country 60 miles (97 km) south of Prince George and 18 miles (29 km) north of Quesnel. It was named 40 years ago by Dr Lloyd Champlain who decided the place could be made into a movie colony. But in spite of much ballyhoo and advertising nothing much came of the venture. About 250 people live in the district and lumbering, mining and farming are now the main industries . . .' To this Mr Bryant added a piquant afterthought: 'P.S. There is a movie show here, three times a week, equipped for Cinemascope.'

Stories of absorbing interest underlie the postmarks of such places as Ultimo (New South Wales, Australia), Medicine Hat (Alberta, Canada), Clemenceau (Arizona, USA), Rugby (Tennessee, USA), Banana (Queensland, Australia), Dynamite Factory (South Africa) and Suwarrow in the South Pacific Cook Islands group.

To take the last-named first, here is an outline of the Suwarrow postmark's background story: In 1969 the Cook Islands' Government announced the opening of a new post office at Suwarrow, a South Pacific atoll, half a mile in length and 300 yards wide (800 m by 270 m), sited 200 miles (220 km) from the nearest inhabited island and 513 miles (820 km) from Rarotonga. About the same time it was reported that Tom Neale, a Wellington-born New Zealander, the only inhabitant of Suwarrow had, on 22 July 1969, been appointed the postmaster of that island. Until that time Mr Neale had acted in a quasi-official capacity as custodian of the island, keeping records of ships calling there and of whale sightings and of the quantity of pearl shell recovered periodically by divers from Manihiki.

Mr Neale had first seen Suwarrow on a two-day visit in 1945.

The place enthralled him, and he resolved to live there some day. The chance to do so occurred seven years later. He disembarked on the 100-acre atoll from the inter-island trader *Mahurangi*, at the age of 50, with two cats and £49 worth of stores on 7 October 1952. He remained alone, with only two visits from passing ships until June 1954 when he was miraculously rescued after injuring his back.

Mr Neale returned to the atoll in April 1960, remaining there until 27 December 1963. Having in the meantime published an enthralling book *An Island to Oneself*, he returned again to Suwarrow in 1968, since when outgoing items of mail stamped with a 'Tom Neale' cachet and the postmark 'Suwarrow, Cook Islands' have enriched the collections of philatelists, cover collectors and cancellation enthusiasts in many distant corners of the world.

The story behind Ultimo's postmark, if less exotic, is by no means banal:

In 1803 a junior official preparing papers for a court martial in Australia made a slight but important error. He wrote 'ultimo' instead of 'instant'. The error, trivial though it was, had some interesting results: without being aware that he had done so the court official had triggered off a sequence of events that led, among other things, to a Sydney suburb being given a most unusual name.

Because of the mistake Dr John Harris, a Sydney surgeon, avoided a great deal of trouble. Born in Moneymore, Ireland, in 1754, Dr Harris had trained for the medical profession and for 10 years served with the navy in Indian waters. Later, as a surgeon's mate in the New South Wales Corps, he arrived at Port Jackson in June 1790 and was stationed at Parramatta. The circumstances in which Dr Harris found himself involved in court martial proceedings are now obscure but the relevant fact is that a lowly official's careless use of the word 'ultimo' invalidated the proceedings. Dr Harris commemorated his fortunate escape in a somewhat extraordinary way. He named his house 'Ultimo' and in the course of time the suburb itself, 2 miles (3·2 km) from Sydney, also adopted the name. Moreover, there is still in Ultimo a thoroughfare—the Government printers' office is sited there—named Harris Street.

A really rare postmark of Ultimo would be one dated 1 July

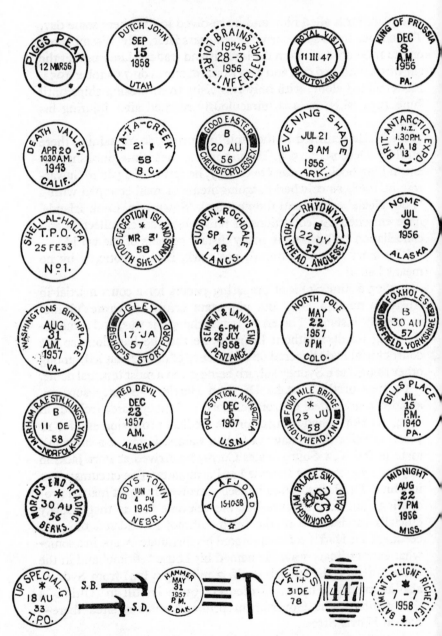

4 *Every postmark tells a story*

1880. That is the date on which its post office first opened. It was closed for a brief period during 1889 and re-opened on 6 January 1890. Dr Harris himself outlived with distinction the episode which put the name of his residence on the map. He died on 27 April 1838 leaving property reputedly worth £150,000.

Like that of Ultimo the name of Medicine Hat is calculated to merit investigation in the pages of any gazetteer. It is a name (to quote Kipling) 'that has no duplicate in the world; it makes men ask questions . . . draws the feet of young towards it; it has powers of uniqueness, individuality, assertion and power. Above all it is the lawful, original, sweat-and-dust won name of the city and to change it would be to risk the luck of the city, to disgust and dishearten the old-timers, not in the city alone, but the world over.'

Why and when did Rudyard Kipling thus express himself on the subject of a rugged community in faraway Alberta? Why this outburst from the great man of letters? It is a long story and one well told by Edward McCourt in his memorable *The Road Across Canada*, published in 1965, and elaborated still further in correspondence made public by E. G. Goodwin, editor of the *Medicine Hat News*.

Briefly, Medicine Hat, Alberta—a city of some 25,000 people on the South Saskatchewan River—may be said to have derived its unusual name from a tradition linked with the headwear of the Indian medicine man.

But there is more to it than that.

At one period about the year 1907, Rudyard Kipling visited the town during a grand trans-Canada tour and was enthralled at the reception he was given by the community's old-timers at the Cypress Club. 'We met him as man to man in all our rustic habits', reported one member of the Club's reception committee. 'We talked to him as if he were a beef-buyer and really had a whale of a time.'

Kipling wallowed in this open-hearted hospitality. He lapped it up and reputedly coined a phrase thereafter used to describe the place: 'The city with all hell for a basement.'

Three years after Kipling's visit brash incomers began to demand that the town's name should be changed. They sought a plebiscite so that a new name—one that would sound 'like a man's best girl'; one that would 'look like business at the head of a financial report'—might be chosen.

The suggestion incensed the old-timers. Through the fluent and persuasive pen of postmaster Frank Fatt they appealed to Kipling—then at the height of his Empire drum-beating fame—to assist their cause. Kipling responded. What, he asked, did men think of a family which, after rising in the world, changed its name for social reasons? What, he wondered, at the end of an impassioned and fiery epistle, should be the name of a city that sold its name for one that 'sounded like a man's best girl?' Perhaps, he hazarded, Judasville would be an appropriate alternative?

Kipling's letter, described as 'a masterpiece of sentiment, satire, logic and invective' completely won the day.

Just as Medicine Hat is linked with an international personality, so, too, is the modest and unassuming copper-mining town of Clemenceau in Yavapai county, Arizona.

Founded in 1920, the town took its name from Georges Benjamin Eugène Clemenceau (1841–1929) the veteran statesman who earned for himself the redoubtable nickname 'Tiger of France'. Tough though he was, Monsieur Clemenceau's sentimental Gallic heart was touched by the fact that a faraway American community had decided to adopt his surname. In his will he bequeathed to the town an ornamental vase 'to be placed in a suitable case in the town's high school'. With Gallic prudence and a sense of life's impermanence, he stipulated that should the town be abandoned at any time the vase was to be returned to France.

Clemenceau's post office was discontinued in the 1950s and when the town itself was eventually abandoned the vase was reportedly returned as requested. But for many years a framed letter from the former Premier hung in a place of honour on the office wall of the district's schools superintendent.

Two references in widely separated sources summarise the extraordinary background story of the postmark of Rugby, Tennessee. The first is an issue of *The Rugby Gazette and East Tennessee News* dated Saturday, 9 May 1885 in which part of an advertisement reads: 'The town of Rugby is beautifully laid out and picturesquely situated between the gorges of Clear Fork River and White Oak Creek. The streets are clean and dry and invalids will find no difficulty in taking exercise even in the worst winter weather. They are bordered by, for the most part, good houses standing in well-kept, neatly-fenced gardens and by several very attractive villa residences.'

The second reference source is a Tennessee state highway marker: 'RUGBY. Five miles west is Rugby, founded 5 October 1880 by Thomas Hughes, author of *Tom Brown's Schooldays*, in an idealistic endeavour to provide homes and livelihood in the United States for the younger sons of English gentry. Within three years the settlement had proved financially impracticable but its English origins are still visible.'

Between these two brief factual references lies a story of high hopes, ambitious plans and wild, impractical optimism. With its postmark as a starting point the collector may discover that an early postmaster at Rugby was Samuel G. ('Uncle Sam') Wilson, who came from England to Tennessee as a young man and served as postmaster and as a lay reader in the settlement's church for 45 years. His proudest boast was that he never shaved and never married. Wilson was followed in more recent times by Miss Nona Smith during whose term as postmistress the post office premises were sited in Kingston Lisle, the impressive house (named after a village in Berkshire, England) which Hughes built for himself but never occupied.

To pinpoint another postmark story one must forsake the old water-wheel grist mills and the log houses and plantation mansions of rural Tennessee and cross the Pacific to the grassy plains and coastal highlands of Queensland, Australia. There, on the Dawson Highway, 95 miles (152 km) from Rockhampton, stands the little town of Banana.

The settlement has a long and honourable history. Its post office was established on 1 September 1861, at which time there were only 24 post offices in the whole of the State. Postmistress Eva Sutherland writes: 'Our town has no banana plantations, and never did have. It's one of the oldest towns in Queensland and 4 miles away we have the Moura coalmine. Our official post office was moved when Banana went into a decline about 30 years ago. My aunt took over a non-official office for 23 years and I used to assist her. Then I took over the office myself.'

How did Banana get its extraordinary name? 'In the old days goods on cattle stations were carted by bullock teams. One old working bullock here was called Banana—he was so soft—and that's how Banana came by its name.'

A postal mark equally intriguing in an entirely different way is that of Dynamite Factory, South Africa. Copies of this postmark dated as early as 1904 have been recorded and it is possible that the post office here—sited some 2½ miles (4 km) from Somerset West, in Cape Province—has existed from the time the factory was established in 1903. In the 1950s the plant was operated by Cape Explosive Works Limited in association with Imperial Chemical Industries and in 1959 it was reported to employ about 2,250 people in the manufacture of explosives of all kinds for mining, sub-soiling and other activities.

Complementary to this double-ring date-stamp would be one from the township of Giant, California, whose post office, listed in 1937 but closed by 1949, was named for the Giant Powder Company of Wilmington, Delaware. The company established a West Coast plant in California in 1880 and 'giant powder' was for many years a popular local name for the dynamite produced there.

From these examples it can be seen that almost any postmark may well have a tale to tell, especially those linked in some tangible way with the lives and hopes and aspirations of *people*.

6
Personal Postmarks

A department of postmark collecting which has been only sparsely explored is that of linking the study with biographical subjects, of which one or two instances were given in the preceding chapter. The stories thus revealed—with a postmark as their focal point— are often of absorbing interest. They may concern statesmen, lawyers, famous women, soldiers, explorers, postmasters, frontiersmen, politicians or humble folk whose names appear on the map purely by some remarkable freak or mischance.

To pursue this theme a little further let us take as an example the postmark of the Australian uranium mining town of Mary Kathleen, located on the Selwyn Range midway between Cloncurry and Mount Isa.

How did Mary Kathleen come to be so named?

The story behind this postmark began in July 1954 when two tough mineral prospectors, Norman McConachy and Clem Walton, were making their way along a dry Queensland creek bed in a truck. The men had an idea that this sparse, sun-blistered scrubland 1,000 miles (1,600 km) from Brisbane might conceal uranium in its rock formations, but so far nothing tangible had come to light to reinforce their hopes. Suddenly the truck jolted to a standstill and while Walton lifted the engine cover to trace the fault his partner sauntered around and idly switched on his geiger counter. The instrument reacted wildly. One of the world's great uranium strikes had been made. Two days later, with their partners in the syndicate, the two men staked their claim. For the syndicate it meant riches. They sold out their claim for £250,000 in cash and a large shareholding in the company formed to work the mine.

For Norman McConachy the lucky strike held heartbreak as

5 *Personal postmarks*

well as happiness: his wife had died only a few weeks earlier. Today this well-planned model township, with its neat houses and wide green lawns, its swimming pool, churches, supermarket and cinema, exists as a lasting memorial to McConachy's wife, Mary Kathleen, after whom it was named.

Personal names of this kind abound on the world map. They can be found in every continent and their postal markings when gathered into an individual collection, concern more human interest stories than the pages of a daily newspaper—provided one is prepared to research their background.

Americans miss few opportunities to name their towns and villages in honour of men and women, some of them internationally famous and others whose achievements have gained only local recognition. This is one reason why American postmarks are so fascinating to collect. They almost always have a worthwhile background story.

Pershing, Oklahoma, is a typical example. Its post office, opened on 31 May 1919, was named as a tribute to General John J. Pershing (1860–1948) who commanded the American expeditionary force in France during the First World War. In the same way McArthur, a town in Vinton County, Ohio, was named in honour of General Duncan McArthur, a hero of the War of 1812. The lives of both these men are well worth closer study.

Even famous nicknames have a role to play in American postal place-name nomenclature. Several towns bear the name Stonewall, honouring 'Stonewall' Jackson, hero of the Civil War Confederate forces, and in Davidson County, Tennessee, the postmàrk of Old Hickory helps to immortalise the nickname of Andrew Jackson, seventh President of the United States, who earned the sobriquet for the tough, uncompromising strength of his personal character.

Rough and Ready, California, is another instance of a nickname which has gained prominence and publication in postmark form. General Zachary ('Rough and Ready') Taylor, son of a Virginian planter and twelfth President of the United States spent much of his life fighting against the Indians and the Mexicans. His nickname was adopted by at least three places in California, but apparently only one of them, in Nevada County, has survived in postmark form. The town of Rough and Ready was founded in

1849 by the Rough and Ready Company, led by Captain A. A. Townsend who had served in the US Army under General Taylor. In the pioneer days of the Californian gold rush Rough and Ready had a population of 5,000 but in 1956 only 130 people lived there.

Mason and Dixon, which to English ears sounds a little like the name of a respectable old-established High Street family store, existed until the 1950s as the name of a post office in Franklin County, Pennsylvania, near a famous state frontier. This boundary was established in 1763–67 by Charles Mason and Jeremiah Dixon, two noted English surveyors. It marked the line which separated the 'free' state of Pennsylvania from the 'slave' state of Maryland and, later, Virginia. The line ran westward from the Delaware and helped to settle a bitter territorial dispute and the postmark which commemorated the names of its originators is now among the comparative rarities in many collections.

From Carter County, Oklahoma, the postmark of Gene Autry recalls a man famed in another sphere. The community lies 10 miles (16 km) northeast of Ardmore and it was formerly known as Berwyn. On 1 January 1942 the little town and its post office were renamed as a tribute to the American singing cowboy Gene Autry, a motion picture actor and composer of about 200 popular songs.

By way of contrast, Monterville, in Randolph County, West Virginia, acquired its name because its postmaster had one to spare. The village was originally called Middlebrook which proved to be unsatisfactory because there were several other places of that name. Then John Ernest Monterville Bing took office as post-master. Bing had always felt that his full name was far too long. He decided to get rid of one of his forenames and applied to the US postal administration to have the name of his post office changed to Monterville. The suggestion was accepted. From that point on the village became Monterville and its postmaster signed himself John Ernest Bing.

Their postal place-names suggest that Americans have a high regard for patriots who fight for freedom, irrespective of their race, creed, colour or nationality.

Behind the postmark of Red Cloud, Webster County, Nebraska lies the story of an Indian chief whose name struck terror into the hearts of his enemies. Red Cloud was the last warrior-chief of the

Teton-Sioux tribe. He was born in 1821 and died on 10 December 1909. In 1860 he led an attack by an Indian raiding party in which 100 soldiers, under Captain Fetterman, were massacred near Fort Phil Kearny. He finally signed a peace treaty with the United States Government in 1880 and, according to local tradition, the town of Red Cloud (population 1,744 in 1955) was built on the site where Red Cloud held a war council.

Further north, in Alaska, the village of Baranof owes its name to a Russian fur-trader who became a governor of one of Russia's overseas possessions. He was Alexander Baranof (1746–1819) who in 1796 founded a colony at Bering Strait. The village which carries Baranof's name is sited at the head of Warm Spring Bay, 19 miles (30 km) from Sitka. Its post office, established in 1907, closed five years later and re-opened in 1917.

Contrasts form an interesting background to a selection of personal name postmarks: an artist may be responsible for one such name; a chocolate manufacturer may be remembered in another.

An English artist gave his name to the American community of Moran, sited at an altitude of 6,742 feet (2043 m) in Teton County, Wyoming. Thomas Moran was a member of the expedition led by Dr F. V. Hayden which in 1871 surveyed parts of Wyoming. The aim of the expedition was to study geology and zoology and make maps of the area. Moran painted many pictures of the region, including a panoramic view of the Grand Canyon. Later this painting was purchased by Congress of the US for $10,000.

In more recent times—in 1937—6,000 workers at his chocolate factory helped Milton Hershey to celebrate his eightieth birthday. The occasion was their opportunity to pay tribute to a man who in 1903 founded America's 'chocolate town'—Hershey, Pennsylvania. The son of Swiss immigrants, Hershey began his own candy-making business in 1876 at the age of 19. After many setbacks he developed a prosperous enterprise and by the early 1920s his factory had trebled in size. From two small buildings the factory has now grown to more than 2 million square feet (200,000 square metres) of floor space in 26 separate buildings. The chocolate town's founder died in October 1945 at the age of 88, but not before he had given his name to a thriving model community and

59

had had the satisfaction of seeing his own name established on the map and distributed far and wide in postmark form.

Canada, too, can provide many examples of personal postmarks which perpetuate the names of prominent people.

Nicolet (Province of Quebec) recalls the name of the great explorer, Jean Nicolet, who was born in 1598. In 1620 Nicolet was sent by Samuel de Champlain, the French governor of Canada, to dwell with the Nipissing tribe of Indians, to learn their language and study their customs. Fourteen years later he explored Lake Michigan and ascended the Fox River into what is now Wisconsin, becoming the first white man to explore that region. Nicolet was drowned near Quebec in 1642 but his name survives in the Canadian town near Trois Rivières.

The freak of fate by which a Canadian city came to bear the name of a seventeenth-century English prince adds piquant interest to another Canadian postmark.

When the western terminus of Canada's Grand Trunk Pacific railroad was completed in 1906, a competition was organised to find an appropriate name for the town at the end of the line. Out of 12,000 names submitted for a 250-dollar prize the name suggested by Miss Eleanor McDonald of Winnipeg was selected as the winner.

Miss McDonald suggested Prince Rupert, the name borne by the Royalist cavalry leader who was a cousin of King Charles II. The relevance of this choice lay in the fact that Prince Rupert, a dashing and romantic figure—an artist and inventor as well as a distinguished leader—was the first governor of the important Hudson's Bay Company.

The postmarks of some communities reveal that they arrived at their eventual choice of a name only after a good deal of trial and error.

The Canadian city of Kitchener (population 95,000) on the Grand River in Ontario, 62 miles (99 km) from Toronto, has had four names since it was founded. It was first known as Sand Hills, and then as Ebytown after Benjamin Eby, a popular Mennonite bishop. After that, for a time, it was known as Berlin. But in a wave of patriotic fervour during the First World War, it took the name of Kitchener as a token of respect for Lord Kitchener, the

British military leader who was drowned while on a mission to Russia in HMS *Hampshire* in 1916.

In the same province the town of Galt received its name as a tribute by one man to his childhood friend. Galt was established in 1816 as a modest settlement on land purchased by the Hon William Dickson, of Niagara. It consisted of a grist-mill, a distillery, a saw-mill and a few houses and it was first known as Shade's Mill. Then Dickson recalled John Galt, a friend of his in Scotland who had once attended the same school. He changed the settlement's name to Galt and in doing so he honoured a man who was destined to become one of Scotland's best-known writers on country life and other topics.

Lloydminster, on the Alberta-Saskatchewan border was the site of a British colony established by the Rev I. M. Barr. Soon after the colony was founded the responsibility for running it was taken over by the Rev George Exton Lloyd, a theological student from Toronto who later became Bishop of Saskatchewan. Lloyd was a leader as well as a scholar. He distinguished himself at the Battle of Cut Knife Hill in 1885 and later his services to the community were acknowledged by linking his name with that of the town.

Dawson, in Canada's North West Territories began its colourful existence as a town site staked in 1896. At the height of the 1898 gold rush its population was estimated at 20,000. Its name, originally Dawson City, is a tribute to George Mercer Dawson (1849–1901) the geologist son of Sir John William Dawson. Dawson served on the staff of the Geological Survey of Canada, becoming its director in 1895. He was in charge of the Yukon expedition in 1887. Ten years later the first post office in Dawson, with Inspector Frank Harper in charge, began to cancel outgoing mail with the name of this eminent Nova Scotian-born geologist and naturalist.

Occasionally the connection between a postmark and the person to whom it relates is of recent or current topical interest and living personalities are sometimes featured in this way.

The memory of Dr Ralph Vaughan Williams, the English composer, was honoured in April 1972 with the issue at his birthplace in Down Ampney, Gloucestershire, of a special commemorative handstamp on the centenary anniversary of his birth. The voyages of round-the-world yachtsmen Sir Francis Chichester and Chay Blyth have been commemorated, during their lifetime, in a similar way. There has always been widespread interest in anniversary handstamps and thousands of prominent persons have been featured in postmarks of this kind (see figure 5).

In Britain, name-links with people, past and present, are more difficult to find on the map than they are in such regions as Australia, Canada and America. But with patience and a little research they can be found.

The postmark of Saltaire, Yorkshire, for example, combines in its name a nineteenth-century wool manufacturer and a northern river. The 'Salt' part of the name derives from Sir Titus Salt (1803–1876) a generous man of great drive and imagination, who was the first to manufacture alpaca fabrics in England. Around his factories in a pleasant valley of the River Aire rose the model village of Saltaire, 4 miles (6 km) northwest of Bradford.

Geographically in a nearby locality is Dunsville, Doncaster, Yorkshire. It was named for a developer called Edward Dunn who founded and built the village in 1932.

Across on the west coast of England the fishing port and seaside resort of Fleetwood carries the family name of a man once well-known in political circles. He was Sir Peter Hesketh Fleetwood, born 1801 at Wennington Hall near Lancaster. The town on the Wyre estuary that bears his name was planned and developed in 1836.

A name even more familiar in international circles is that of the wartime British premier, Sir Winston Churchill, who died in 1965. The Churchill name is echoed many times in various parts of the world, including a Somerset village in the lee of the Mendips and a town in Manitoba, Canada, named in the seventeenth-century for Governor Sir John Churchill. A more recently opened post office which bears the Churchill name is sited in a Royal Navy married quarters estate at Helensburgh, Scotland. It was opened on 13 August 1968 and named for Sir Winston Churchill.

Robin Hood, the legendary English outlaw, has a place on the map and a postmark to honour his memory in the Yorkshire village of Robin Hood, near Wakefield. Apart from the fact that a local school has its Sherwood House, the connection with the romantic outlaw of Sherwood Forest is allowed to go almost unremarked, but there is also an East Coast village called Robin Hood's Bay.

Three other personalities of differing background whose names appear on English postmarks are Queen Adelaide, Thomas Telford and Peter Lee.

Queen Adelaide, born 1792, married William, Duke of Clarence who in 1830 became King of Great Britain and Ireland under the style of William IV. In Cambridgeshire her name survives as that of a village near Ely.

Thomas Telford, the British civil engineer, is a relatively recent recruit to the postmark Hall of Fame. The Shropshire town named after him was created under an order of the Minister of Housing and Local Government issued on 13 December 1968. Designed to take the overspill population from the West Midlands conurbation, the the town will eventually accommodate some 230,00 people, an estimated population increase of some 10,000 a year. Several types of Telford postal markings are in use. Appropriately, they honour the son of a Dumfriesshire shepherd who in 1787 became a surveyor of public works for Shropshire and as a tribute to whose memory many fine roads and bridges exist to this day in various parts of Britain.

Peterlee (County Durham, England) is such a natural-sounding postal place-name that one never thinks of it as deriving from a personal name source. It is one of several New Towns planned in 1948 as the basis for a model residential community. Its population (298 in 1951) had grown to 17,963 by 1965. The name it bears is that of Peter Lee, social worker and one-time president of the Miner's Federation, who died in 1935.

In every part of the world postal place-names of this kind invite the attention of the thematic postmark collector. Cradock, South Africa, was named for Sir John Cradock, the Irish-born son of a Dublin archbishop who saw service against Napoleon in Egypt and later became a governor of the Cape of Good Hope. Theron, in Orange Province, South Africa, commemorates a Boer Scout, Daniel Theron, who served in the South African War and was killed in action in 1900.

The name of a French ambassador is recalled by the postmark of Choiseul on the mountainous West Indian island of St. Lucia, in the Windward Group. The island's post office was opened in

1885 and the settlement was named for the Duc de Choiseul-Amboise (1719–1785) an eminent French statesman who became his country's Foreign Minister in 1758.

On the other side of the world and at the other end of the social scale, the postmark of a South Pacific island perpetuates the name of an otherwise unknown French seaman who happened to have good eyesight. He was Joseph Raoul, quartermaster of a vessel captained by Bruni D'Entrecasteaux, a French admiral who explored the region near New Guinea in the 1790s. Quartermaster Raoul was the first man to sight the island and the commander named it in his honour. Raoul Island, in the Kermadec group, is also known as Sunday Island and it is administered by the Government of New Zealand.

Women, and their personal names, are by no means neglected or ignored in postmark form. The background story of Hobhouse, South Africa, was outlined in chapter 5. In other parts of the world place-name tributes have been accorded to women from many varied walks of life.

Belva (West Virginia) pays homage to Belva Lockwood, a pioneer feminist born at Royalton, New York, in 1830. She studied law and was admitted to the Bar at Washington in 1873. In 1879 she secured passage of a law admitting women to practise in the Supreme Court and was twice (1884 and 1888) a candidate for the presidency of the United States.

Annette (Alaska) was named in 1879 by W. H. Dall of the US Coast and Geodetic Survey for his wife, Annette Whitney Dall. Dacono (Colorado) was named for three women, by combining the first letters of their names: Daisy, Cora and Nona.

Helen Keller's name has appeared in a postmark from Israel; Florence Nightingale has been featured on British handstamps, and Jenny Lind, the Swedish singer, was remembered in postmark form on mail passing through the post office of Jenny Lind in Calaveras County, California, until the office closed in the 1950s. Many other women, famous and unknown, have been given recognition by having places named for them

Rising Fawn (Georgia, USA) is an attractive name derived from that of a Cherokee Indian princess. Owatonna (Minnesota, USA) was reputedly the daughter of a mighty Indian chief named

Wabena; Ladismith, Lady Brand, Lady Frere, Lady Grey and Ladysmith (all in South Africa) were named for the wives of personalities prominent in the republic's nineteenth-century history.

In South Australia, Caroline was reputedly named for the daughter of Governor Daly; Carrietown for a daughter of Governor Sir William Jervois; Elliston for a Miss Ellen Liston, and Elizabeth—a model city 17 miles (27 km) north of Adelaide, planned and built since 1954—was named in honour of the British Queen Elizabeth II, while Adelaide itself was named by Royal command after the consort of King William IV.

Even Willowmore, a name apparently unassociated with personal postmarks, has a direct link with the subject: the name, that of a South African town established in 1862, was chosen by a farmer who combined his wife's maiden name (More) with that of a willow tree growing nearby.

These are some of the fascinating byways into which a study of personal postmarks may lead one. The subject, as far as the present writer is aware, has never been fully exploited, yet its possibilities are as fascinating as they are limitless.

To develop a specialised collection of this kind would require patience, energy, research and inquiry. It could include autographed examples of the British 'free franking' system, established in the seventeenth century, when the privilege of free postage was accorded to members of both Houses of Parliament; it could also embrace the personalised postmasters' provisional stamps issued in the United States from 1845 until the issue of national stamps there in July 1847. To gather a collection along these lines, on the personal postmarks theme, would be a pleasant pursuit of compelling interest and a source of immeasurable pleasure and satisfaction to its compiler.

7
Postmarks Rare
and Interesting

The specialist collector in any field is seldom content to let things drift. He will always have an alert, discerning eye for material of aesthetic and perhaps historic appeal and for specimens which accord with his own special preferences rather than those to which the casual enthusiast is drawn. People of this calibre are constantly setting new trends and standards which tend eventually to enliven and enrich the whole collecting scene.

As a confirmed postmark enthusiast one shared for example, in 1948, the zeal with which the notable British postmarks authority Captain F. C. Holland reported the discovery of a very rare Pearson Hill cancellation of 1857: a type probably in use only for a few days and of which few copies were deemed to exist.

One admires the scholarly patience with which that doyen of American collectors, the late Dr Howard K. Thompson, outlined with impressive clarity a proposed classification system for US handstamped postmarks in the December 1940 issue of *The American Philatelist*. Subsequently he continued to add so much to his fellow collectors' knowledge and appreciation of the whole subject of postal markings. Dr Thompson's personal collection of postmarks and allied material totalled over 700,000 catalogued items, accommodated in 300 carefully indexed volumes. His death in April 1972 at the age of 79 was a great loss to the postmark collecting fellowship.

In his study of country and postmaster markings he outlined a preliminary general classification within 22 different categories embracing, for example, the size of circles, colours, type of obliterator and other factors. Elsewhere in the world, specialists in various areas of postal history have made significant contributions to an understanding and appreciation of the postmarks subject.

Against this background, armed with this knowledgeable research material, one may enjoy the thrill of auction catalogue browsing, especially when one finds within the lists such items as: '*Lot 136*. Napoleonic War, 1803–15: 1803 holograph E.L. from Lord Nelson to "Lady Hamilton, Merton Surrey". The letter is dated 20 June 1803 and says, "My dear Emma, I am now in the passage of the Pharo, Charles is with me and Captain Capel says behaves very well. I dare not say more for I never expect you will receive this letter from your ever most affectionate . . . "' (This letter, unsigned, was probably carried to England in a man-of-war and posted in the London Twopenny Post as indicated by a hand-struck large 'w' in a circular frame in red. It featured in a postal history auction in December 1945 at a valuation of £35.)

Or this: '*Lot 160*. 1700 (*circa*). A collection of entires complete with letter bearing impressions of the second type (sans serif letters) of Bishopmark introduced in 1673 . . . all conveyed on the Great North Road between London and Edinburgh. Twelve letters in a folder . . . '

Or this, of more recent date: '*Lot 295*. Pioneer Flights. Including Allahabad Exhibition 1911; six GB 1911 London to Windsor cards; two USA 1912 cards; two Darmstadt cards with special air post stamps; Swiss 1913 card; Hungary 1920 and Vallancey souvenir army post card of 1918 . . . '

High calibre material of this kind helps to add lustre and distinction to the hobby. But to dwell only on the classics of bygone days, many of which are beyond the reach and price range of average collectors, is to ignore much of interest and value on a relatively more accessible level.

In the author's own collection are several British items of interest acquired between the mid-1960s and early 1970s at modest cost. They include:

(*a*) A fine condition entire with letter headed Doctors Common, 20 November 1766, addressed to Mr William Utten, proctor at Norwich, with a fine clear Bishopmark for 20/No.

(*b*) An entire complete with letter, addressed to Sir Wm Lee, Bart; Col 25 Light Dragoons, Craig's Court, Charing Cross, London, dated 25 March 1800. The letter begins: 'Having wrote to you some time ago, and not receiving your answer, I have this day paid your promissory note into the bank of Sir Christopher Sykes and Co which I hope you will not fail to pay . . . '

(*c*) A four-page letter, addressed to Mr Edward Hardy, Villa Keyrine del Huasco, South America, dated 18 August 1827, backstamped 'Bedale', with straight-line arrival postmark 'Chile' in red.

(*d*) An entire complete with letter dated Ossett, Yorkshire, 20 November 1835 addressed to Mr Tiler, Wem, Salop, and beginning: 'My dear Uncle, We are quite prepared to enter into your feelings and sympathise with you under your troubles, as we ourselves are suffering just in the same way . . . '

These are not important items but they provide an interesting link with the past, often supplying first-hand comment on social and economic conditions of the day, in addition to information on contemporary postal rates and routes.

One such letter in the author's own collection is date-lined 'Dublin 24 September 1798'. (See figure II.) A classic of its kind, it reads as follows:

Dear Brother,
Sir Boyle and I had a very good journey, and on our arrival at Chester, met the joyfull news of the defeat of the French Invaders, the Town was at the same time crowded with the Worcestershire Militia which had Volunteerd the Service to Ireland, and I fear had a bad March to Liverpool and Voyage to Ireland in the frightfull storm of Wednesday ye 12th. We providentially avoided that Storm by not arriveing at Holyhead Till the next Evening and embarking the same night (after a tedious Voyage) we landed in Dublin on Saturday morning ye 15th, and made our appearance at the Castle to the utter astonishment of our Servants and our friends in Dublin.

The next day we went down to the Black Rock where we enjoy those Comforts which we were prepareing for ourselves, before the breaking out of the Rebellion, and which were fortunately preservd to us by not finding a Tennant for our House.

I have the satisfaction to say that Sir Boyle is infinitely better for his Journey is in high Spirits and gains Strength every day.

On our road a little on the other side of Chester we met a Chaise with a Coronet, drawn by four Horses which we learnd Conveyd the Earl of Fitzwilliam on his return from Ireland. He had slept at Conway on his way there, on Friday ye 7th and again at the same Inn on Monday ye 10th on his way home. He was but a few hours in Dublin and the same Ship which brought him conveyd him back the next Tide.

The French Officers were one day in Dublin as Prisoners of War after our arrival. They were confind in a Hotel in a Street in a fashionable part of the Town, and the Curiosity of the fine Ladies carryd them to stop in their Carriages under their Windows, to stare at them and when they had the Complaisance to come forward to show themselves, the fair Ladies showd their sensibility of their attention by Bowing to them.

I suppose they were better pleasd with the Ladies than with their Allies of the Irish Union, on whom they liberally bestowd the Epithets of Poltrons Voleur, Assassin and Sauvage in their Conversations with Lord Dillon and some Gentlemen of Rank who were allowd to visit them. These Gentlemen it was remarkable they addressd in the Old Forms of Milford and Monsieur etc. The Ladies discribe Genl Humbert and another of them as being very handsome and well dress'd, powder'd and quene'd. I wish I was sure they were all fairly gone, as it is beleivd that several, both officers and privates, remain about Killalla and in the County of Sligo with the Rebells who still have the Bishop of Killalla and his family in their power.

A few days ago we were Electrified by the news of another French Invasion which provd only to be the descent of Napper Tandy, who finding that his allies were defeated made off. The Invasion of Genl Napper Tandy, I should compare to that of Harlequin if it was not a Melancholy proof that the French

Frigates can at all times and in all places land Men on our Coasts in Spight of all the Efforts of our Cruisers to prevent them.

One should hope that the Irish would be soon tired of their French allies, as they were treated by them with the utmost contempt, not being allowd to Encamp near them, and were punishd by them with hanging shooting and whipping for Murder, Robbery and Maurauding. This Conduct was probably persued by the French to Concilliate the Lord Lieut and Army to whom they knew (that unless their manouvre of a forc'd March to Dublin should succeed) they must unavoidably surrender.

Our attention is at present engag'd by the Rebell Genl Holt formerly a Constable who is at the head of a numerous body of Robbers and Freebooters in the County of Wicklow. This Fellow is about everywhere and had the audacity to come alone into Dublin a few days ago where he was known and near being taken if he had not gallopd off full speed.

Lord Cornwallis is endeavouring to surround him with a numerous Army which is marching and counter marching in all directions.

A considerable body of Troops were billeted in the Black Rock last night and we learnd this morning at the Castle (where we stayd yesterday and now are) that five Militia Officers took possession of our House last night and that three of them slept in our Bed, and declard they had not been so comfortable for a length of time as they had nothing better than Straw to sleep upon. The English Militia are highly commended for their good behaviour in the Houses where they are Billetted. They always make their Beds and Sweep out their Rooms and leave them in a Condition of Cleanliness which astonishes the Irish House Maids.

Sir Boyle joins me in best Love to yourself, Lady Frankland and the charming Emily.

I am Dear Brother,
Ever affectly,
Yours,
   Mary Roche

This fascinating document, bearing a wax seal and imprinted with a circular handstamp reading SE 24 98, was written by Lady Mary Roche, sister of Admiral Sir Thomas Frankland, of Great Thirkleby Hall, Yorkshire, and wife of Sir Boyle Roche (1743–1807) the Irish politician. Sir Boyle, a witty speaker, sat in the Irish Parliament from 1777 until the Union in 1801. He received a baronetcy in 1782 for his support of the government and is famous for his 'bulls'—ludicrous inconsistencies of speech sometimes said to be the special prerogative of Irishmen. Often, it is said, he sent the British House of Commons into shoals of laughter by his witty and eccentric way of expressing himself.

Lady Mary's letter, quoted here in full, is interesting also for its use of the word 'electrified' in the context: ' . . . a few days ago we were electrified by the news of another French invasion . . . '

Material of this kind can still be acquired quite readily through dealers and by exchange with one's fellow members in clubs and societies, as well as by patient search and inquiry in non-philatelic channels. But the collector should try to avoid a tendency to set a value only upon that which is rare and almost unobtainable from the past—while tending to neglect contemporary material which, with discernment, can be obtained with comparative ease and is likely to be of considerable interest in the future.

There are, for example, sections of the collecting fraternity which deplore the current world-wide outpouring of special handstamps in commemoration of what are said, by some, to be trivial events. It could be that this view will not be taken in 30 years' time by collectors who try to acquire some of these 'trivial' mementos.

Almost any postmark which is no longer readily available may come within the classification of being rare and interesting.

To a specialist in the cancellations of Ethiopia the postmark of Entotto could be a rapturous acquisition; to a Bahamas enthusiast the name Wilson City might have an agreeable sound; to an expert on Egyptian cancellations a 'strike' of Seamen's Home, Alexandria might be attractive; to an enthusiast in Danish material the postmark of Gammel Skagen (now known as Højen) might give cause for rejoicing, and to someone who is building a comprehensive collection of Scottish postal markings the sight of a handstamp used in 1910 at an air meeting at Lanark Grand Stand could provoke a rapturous response. Yet none of these scarce and interesting cancellations might appeal to a collector whose area of interest is Nicaragua and whose aim is to acquire an I.S. type cancellation of San Juan del Sur. As has been previously pointed out, in this field we all have our own sense of values.

Three postmarks for which the present writer has a mild affection are imprinted on covers of comparatively recent date. The first is a clear impression of War, West Virginia, USA—an insignificant item except for the fact that it bears the precise date, 3 September 1939, on which Britain and France declared war on Germany, marking for these countries, the fateful beginning of the Second World War.

The second and third closely related items are, respectively, a handstamp, in violet ink, of the small town of Victory, in Essex County, Vermont, USA, and a Burma 'Exptl P.O. No 36' handstamp on a cover to a Rangoon addressee. The respective cancellation dates on these two covers are 8 May 1945 and 15 August 1945—the first being VE-day and the second VJ-day. (See figure XVIII.)

Redirected covers often carry significant detail. One such item, bearing a British King George V penny stamp left Ealing, London, on 2 September 1913 in search of 'Charles G. Hewitt, apprentice, SS *Queensland Transport*, Batavia, Java'. Its subsequent travels included a call at Ocean Island, abortive visits to Osaka and Singapore, and a wide range of date-stamp endorsements authenticated visits to various parts of the East Indies.

A similar cover, featured in the March 1972 edition of a British dealer's catalogue, began its travels at Kayes, French Sudan, on 25 September 1923 and acquired no less than 13 cancellations in the course of its travels during the ensuing 6 months.

Another much-travelled cover was the subject of a competition in a British philatelic magazine during the Second World War. The envelope addressed to Mr S. H. Ahmed at Kabuli Gate, Bombay, India had passed from one address to another in relentless pursuit of the elusive Mr Ahmed. Eventually, almost black with superimposed cancellations, the envelope had given up this fruitless attempt to get itself delivered. Ten years after the start of its extraordinary journey it became the subject of a wartime competition in aid of the British Red Cross and St John's Ambulance Fund. Entrants were offered a prize for correctly estimating the number of postmarks, or part postmarks, shown on a photographic reproduction of the cover.

In 1924, an Italian citizen mailed a Christmas greetings card to an acquaintance in Mexico. The card was successively redirected to Los Angeles—and finally to its destination, Mexico City. The journey occupied 42 years and the card was eventually delivered in November 1966.

Many quite conventional cancellations are of special interest because of the source from which they derive. The Antarctic bases of Argentina, Australia and USA, for example, have provided interesting material as have the postal services of such remote and unusual places as Pitcairn Island, Tristan da Cunha, the Sea Floor Post Office (Bahamas) and the 1965 Indian Mount Everest expedition. Often, these cancellations fall within a thematic category. As such, some of them will be dealt with in the chapter 12, 'Collecting by Theme'.

On balance, the range and variety of worthwhile material is almost unlimited. As town and village cancellations vanish or become rare because of sophisticated systems of postal concentration it is quite possible that special handstamps of various kinds will tend to take their place. It seems probable that many of today's taken-for-granted items may attain a greatly enhanced value and reputation in the course of a decade or two.

8
Eccentric Circles

In this chapter we can, perhaps, deal with errors and oddities in postmark form. For a start, the mis-spelling of place-names occurs more frequently than one might expect. In Britain St Neots is known in modern times to have appeared as St Noets; Codford (Wiltshire) has taken the form Godford; Paignton (Devon) has been recorded as Paington; North Broomhill (Northumberland) has appeared with a missing 'h' and Llanarth in Wales was once postally assigned to Cardingshire, an erroneous form of Cardiganshire. In 1964 a handstamp impression from Baldock, Hertfordshire rendered the place-name as Baldook. Rotherham (Yorkshire) has appeared as Rotheram, and Middlesbrough, in the same county, as Middlesborough. In 1909 a handstamp from the Herefordshire village of Much Marcle gave the post town spelling of Gloucester in the form Glouoester and in 1971 a special handstamp commemorating a Civil War pageant at Warwick encountered trouble with the spelling of siege and went on record with the wording 'Civil War Pageant commemorating the 1642 seige of Warwick Castle'.

However, the modern spelling of place-names is often different from that adopted in bygone days and this fact accounts for many apparent discrepancies on correspondence of the seventeenth, eighteenth and nineteenth centuries. Thus Aylesbury (Buckinghamshire, England) was Aylsbury in 1842 and Rugeley (Staffordshire, England) was Rudgeley in 1806. Hutton Buscel—a village in the North Riding of Yorkshire—appeared in that form until as recently as 1959 when the spelling was changed to Hutton Bushel; Kirbymoorside, also in Yorkshire, inserted an additional letter into its postmark and became Kirkby Moorside on 1 September 1967.

Around the world other places have had trouble with their names in postmark form. On one occasion Braes-River, a Jamaican postmark, mysteriously took the form Braze River and Singapore, postally maltreated, became Snigapore. In 1948 Athabaska (Alberta, Canada) cancelled outgoing mail with the name so spelled. By November 1950 a change of heart, or at least a change of spelling, had occurred and the place-name became Athabasca.

Smith Falls—or Smiths Falls, or Smith's Falls—(Ontario, Canada) underwent even more harrowing changes at the hands of postal officials. In 1937 the postmark was Smith's Falls. In February 1950 it had become Smith Falls but by December of the same year it reverted to Smiths Falls, this time without the apostrophe. Another Canadian error occurred when the slogan THE POSTMAN IS YOUR BEST SALESMAN appeared with the final word in the form SALEMAN.

Occasionally cancellations can be found where numerals representing the date have been inserted in manuscript. This was done, especially in parts of New Zealand and America, when the type had been misplaced. Often the postmasters had to pay for the replacement type and a New Zealand correspondent told how a postmaster once claimed that mice had carried off the missing items.

On 2 January 1958 Assawoman, a curiously named town in Virginia, USA was using a double-ring date-stamp with the name spelt as quoted above. The following day a single-ring handstamp was in use and this time the name was rendered as Asawoman. Even Homer nods: a handstamp from the town of that name—in Georgia, USA—appeared with inverted numerals in 1960 recording the year as 0961!

New Zealand has had its own share of postal place-name mishaps. A cancellation of May 1971 rendered Tataraimaka in the shortened form Tatarimaka and Herald Island appeared as Heralad Island for a short period in 1955. Another troublesome spelling involvement caused a Dominion sea scout event at Lake Waihola to be recorded in postmark form with the erroneous spelling 'Regetta'.

Date errors are frequent—and understandable. Local conditions, even emergencies, may account for a number of postmark freaks. There may be, it is as well to remember, a typhoon raging outside the local post office or a civil disturbance taking place in the piazza half a mile away. Flood waters may be endangering the whole community or the postmaster's wife may be having a baby. Amid distractions of this kind the man in charge of date-stamp operations might be forgiven if he overlooked the fact that September has only 30 days or that the date-stamp device has lost a consonant. In varying conditions such as these, and amid the unending obligation to keep the mail moving, it is not surprising that occasional postmark oversights come into the hands of collectors.

Accidents of one kind or another produce most of these errors, and they are usually quickly rectified. Occasionally, however, one mistake can lead to another. During the year 1918 letters passing through the West Norfolk village of Helhoughton, England, bore the date-stamp Elhoughton. From correspondence in the possession of collectors it is evident that the error escaped unnoticed for some considerable time. By October 1918, however, the mystery of the missing 'H' had evidently been solved and the consonant was reinstated in its rightful place. In Helhoughton, alas, the rejoicing was shortlived. Date-stamp impressions bearing the date 7 October 1918 and the incorrect spelling Helhaughton began to appear!

Such happenings, though rare, are by no means unique. Date-stamp imprints have been known where the place-names have been inverted, reversed and omitted. On one occasion the numerals 1899 were inserted upside down so that a number of astonished addressees received items of correspondence which had apparently been 33 years in transit. In Dunfermline, Scotland on 2 Jan 1969 a cancelling machine franked outgoing mail with the date 6961 and from March, Cambridgeshire in 1960 outbound mail carried the date 31 February.

Mention of freak postmarks would not be complete without a reference to the kicking mule cancellations devised in the 1880s by an eccentric character named Klinkner and the almost equally stylish handstamps of John William Hill and Edmond S. Zevely.

Klinkner, a native of Oakland, California, manufactured metal signs, rubber stamps and similar devices and was eventually persuaded to make cancellers for the postmasters of certain American postal centres including Susanville, Forbestown, Goleta and Port

Eccentric Circles

6 *Eccentric circles*

Townsend. His cancellers took the form of a kicking mule with ears and tail and hind legs raised. They took the fancy of collectors as long ago as 1886 and specimens have since been sought by people in all parts of the world.

Several different types of unusual hand-cancellers were in use at Waterbury, Connecticut from about 1865 to 1869 (with occasional examples of later use) and these are attributed to John William Hill (1836–1921) a clerk at Waterbury post office whose postmarks became philatelically famous on account of their unusual subjects and unorthodox design. The cancellers were cut from cork and featured such subjects as a running chicken, an eagle, an elephant, a heart (for St Valentine's Day) and a clown's head (for use on 1 April). The United States postal authorities expressed disapproval of Hill's cancellers on the grounds that they were not sufficiently dignified for official use, but examples of his work are now highly prized.

Edmond S. Zevely's handstamps are also well known. Described as a lively and wide-awake man, Zevely was appointed postmaster at Pleasant Grove, in Alleghany County, Maryland when the post office there was established on 19 December 1849. His 'manufactory' for the production of post office stamps, wood types and proof presses is recorded in a gazetteer of 1852 and here he produced cancellers in many strange and original designs.

Covers bearing Zevely's handstamps, like those bearing the impressions of Klinkner and Hill, are now widely sought and are considered to be rare and valuable in philatelic circles around the world.

In a peripheral sense also within the category of postmark freaks and eccentric circles are the philatelic gymnastics performed by some collectors. One of these, a Mrs H. F. Simons of Willoughby, Ohio, USA amassed a collection of 30,000 American postmarks, gathered in a period of 12 years. With this material at her disposal Mrs Simons contrived on one occasion to write a 1000-word travelogue using only postmarks as her means of narration.

About the same period, the American magazine *Collier's Weekly* offered 25-dollar awards for each published picture postmark contribution to its columns—the aim being to arrange genuine postmarks in such a manner as to create a sentence or an idea. Actual postmarks had to be submitted and there were many astonishing entries.

Using five different postmarks one ingenious entrant devised the phrase ONLY (Tenn.) ALERT (Ind.) CROOKS (S. Dak.) LOCATE (Mont.) MONEY (Miss.). Another contributor contrived the comment HI HAT (Ky.) SMITHS TURN OUT (S.C.) TOBE (Col.) ORDINARY (Ky.). Yet another competitor managed to express in postmark form the succinct comment FERTILE (Iowa) ACRES (Kansas) PRODUCE (Florida) PREMIUM (Ky.) CORN (Okla.).

Serious students of postal history may not approve of such light-hearted activities but at least it can be said that they promote interest in the subject, encourage ingenuity and make a pleasant change.

9
The Regional Collection

One great advantage of postmark and cover collecting is the ease with which it is possible to specialise in material from a single, selected region. There are virtually no limits to the areas available for study. A small village or town would suffice if one wished to confine the study to a compact and concentrated area; conversely a continental region would not be too large if one wished to pursue a more superficial review.

Here is a random selection from the titles of some of the articles, monographs and books which have appeared in recent years. Each one pinpoints some region, large or small, whose postmarks and postal history have been considered worthy of attention:

Ceylon: Early Postmarks and Postal History
Postal Markings of Newfoundland
Hong Kong Post Offices and Cancellations
Perou, Obliterations Postales
South African Postmarks
Postal Markings of the Nord Départment, France
The Mileage Marks of Devon
New South Wales Numeral Cancellations
The Postal History of the Yukon Territory
Chinese Tibetan Postmarks
The Postal Markings of Barbados
The Greek Post Offices and their Postmarks
The Post Offices and Cancellations of Fiji
Cancellation Study of the British Solomon Islands Protectorate
Sarawak Postal Markings
Danish Postmarks

ADELAIDE, AUG. 23rd 1972
OFFICIAL SOUVENIR COVER

IX *Commemorative covers, Canada, Australia Great Britain*

THE POSTAL HISTORY SOCIETY
CONFERENCE
BURY
1
PAID
30 SEPT 1972
BURY ST EDMUNDS

50th Anniversary
Calgary Stampede
JULY 9 - 14, 1962

1912 - 1962

Souvenir cover by
BRITISH-AMERICAN COLLECTORS' CLUB
725-15th Street N.W., Calgary, Alberta, Canada

CALGARY
3 PM
9 VII
1962
ALBERTA

DAWSON CITY CANADA
GOLD RUSH
FESTIVAL
JULY 1 - AUG 25

The Editor,
The Stamp Magazine,
Link House,
Store Street,
LONDON, W.C.1,
ENGLAND.

FESTIVAL
MOOMBA
1960
STAMP DISPLAY
MELBOURNE

MOBILE POST OFFICE
MOOMBA FESTIVAL
12 MAR 60
1960
MELBOURNE-VIC AUS

K. A. ROBERTSON
188 SPRINGFIELD-RD.
BLACKBURN.

The Regional Collection

The Postmarks of Gambia
Current Post Offices and Postmarks of the Cayman Islands
The Welsh Post Towns Before 1840
Postmarks of Falkland Islands Dependencies Survey Bases
The Postmarks of Brazil
Postmarks of the Kingdom of Yemen

The regional scope of these studies extends, as will be seen, from a specialised and finite study of a particular type of postmark in a relatively confined region in the west of England to an overall survey of the postmarks of a vast land area such as Brazil. Could anything more accurately indicate the enormous, world-wide scope of the subject?

To be even more specific, here is an extract from one of the author's previously published articles dealing with a selection of modern postmarks from a typical region—Alaska:

'The story of Alaska has been told and retold many times. The name itself derives from the Aleut word "al-ay-ek-shya" meaning "mainland" and the State's early history as Russian America and, later, as the scene of the great gold rush of the 1890s makes heroic and colourful reading.

'The admission of this vast land and water region of 586,400 square miles (1,520,000 km²) into the American Union as the 49th state was announced by President Eisenhower on 3 January 1959. Alaska's postmarks bring many episodes of its history into close focus. As a region it is rich in material. As at 1 July 1967 there were 203 post offices in the state, and almost every one of them has a story worth recording. Here is postmistress Lillian McGlashan writing from Akutan, Alaska in September 1956: "There are no Eskimos or Indians here: the natives are Aleuts, and our village, the largest in the Aleutian chain mail-route has a population of 104."

'Or, graphically, from Point Hope comes this message from an Eskimo postmaster: "We get polar bear during winter, on ice. Ice boat shut travel early November. We get walrus in spring and caribou 5 miles (8 km) from village. Caribou eat lichen food and good swimmers riding high in water."

'Other letters and notes and post card messages speak of mighty glaciers such as the mammoth Mendenhall Glacier near Juneau,

81

of farming in the Tanana valley and of logging operations for the pulp and lumber mills on Prince of Wales Island in south-eastern Alaska.'

Many of these quaintly phrased notes and messages are from Eskimos, Alaska's best-known native people, who live much as their ancestors did hundreds of years ago.

Again, curious place-names, always fascinating to the postmark collector, abound throughout the state. Gold Rush, an appropriate name, is a station of Fairbanks. Fish Egg (now Craig) had a post office about 60 miles (96 km) from Ketchikan. Chicken, in eastern Alaska near the Yukon border, was a gold-mining camp whose post office was established in 1903. There are two explanations of this unusual name. Alice Lawyer, American place-names specialist, says it may derive from the fact that gold found here was in the shape of corn, or chicken feed. But chicken was also a local name for the ptarmigan which frequent the area and are sometimes referred to as 'chicken of the Flats'. Whatever the source of the name, Chicken is an inconsiderable place in terms of population. According to a 1965 road map only 20 people live there.

College (population 1,750) near Fairbanks takes its name from the University of Alaska; and Circle, on the Yukon River 130 miles (208 km) ENE of Fairbanks, was founded in 1894 and so named because its founders supposed it to be exactly on the Arctic Circle. In fact it is many miles south of the Circle, on the Yukon Flats. 'At one time,' wrote postmaster Fred Vogel in 1956, 'Circle was the largest log cabin city in the world, with over 10,000 people.' But in 1964 only 41 people made it their hometown.

Circle Springs, further south, takes its name from the natural springs which flow at a rate of 400 gallons (1,800 litres) a minute at a temperature of 139°F (59°C). A letter from a resident there, some years ago, said that the hot water was used in a local hotel capable of accommodating 160 guests. In the interior of the hotel a temperature of 70°F (21°C) or more could be maintained when the outside thermometer was as low as 72°F below freezing point.

From Clam Gulch post office, Frances Osmer wrote: 'Our post office is near a gulch where there are a number of good clam beds. Old timers called the area Clam Gulch long before the post office came into being in 1950.'

Thus, item by item, one may piece together the background story of a postal place-name. Pelican, on kite-shaped Chichagof Island, derives from a fishing craft owned by an early settler. Red Devil, whose post office was set up in October 1957, takes its name from the Red Devil mining camp. Russian Mission, in western Alaska, stems from the mission established there by the Russian Orthodox Church in 1843. The village stands on the Yukon River, 100 miles (160 km) north of Bethel, and in 1967 about 140 people lived there.

The list of attractive place names is legion. Platinum, Poorman—named for Poorman Creek—Holy Cross, where a Jesuit mission was sited, Ruby and Summit are typical. Mastodon, Lucky Shot, Igloo and King Salmon—these, alone, provide the starting point for a fascinating excursion into Alaskan lore and history.

Even a comparatively simple name like Nome has attractive possibilities. A former gold-rush town on the north shore of Norton Sound, it was founded in 1899 and first known as Anvil City. It appears that the British survey ship *Herald* visited the region and at what is now known as Cape Nome the cartographer wrote 'Name ?' intending to have the accepted name inserted later, when confirmed. However, when the rough map was copied a draughtsman transcribed the scrawled query as Nome. And that, if the story has credence, is why the name appears on the Alaskan map.

Another unusual postmark source is that of North Pole, Fairbanks, where the post office is made of metal and shaped like an igloo. An incorporated town of 600 people North Pole consisted, in 1967, of a school, a cafe, a trailer court, two service stations, two taverns and a trading post.

At one time it was reported that the town's mayor, Con Miller, helped to handstamp 200,000 Christmas letters bearing the North Pole postmark.

Some of the most interesting material from this region comprises covers—especially those mailed between 1943 and 1946—connected with the Alaska Dog Team Post. Typical sets in this category carry the postmarks of Tanana, Minto, Teller, Rampart and Hot Springs with departure and arrival handstamps and, in

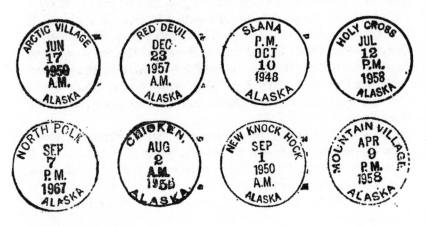

7 *Selection from Alaska*

8 *Borderline postmarks*

many instances, the signatures of postmasters of these Arctic outposts.

By way of contrast quite a different, but no less fruitful, picture could emerge if one were to take as the basis for a postmark study such a region as Gibraltar, pre-1939 Estonia, Thailand, the English county of Yorkshire, the Pacific Cook Islands, or the city of Wagga Wagga, Australia.

Official sources can be, and often are, extremely helpful to the compiler of a local history with a postal background. To take a particular instance let us examine one aspect of the public relations service available from the Historical Office of the Australian Postmaster-General's Department.

Among the facilities offered by this department are a series of well-researched histories of individual Australian post offices. Here are extracts from a detailed case history of one such place, the world-famous city of Wagga Wagga, New South Wales:

WAGGA WAGGA

It is recorded that Captain Charles Sturt and his party passed over the site of the future town of Wagga Wagga on the banks of the Murrumbidgee River, in 1829.

Settlement followed and Wagga Wagga was destined to become the hub of a huge grazing and pastoral district and an important shopping place midway between Sydney and Melbourne.

The town, proclaimed in 1849, became a city in 1946.

The name Wagga Wagga, according to the council of the city, was derived from the aboriginal language and meant 'Crows, or place where crows assemble in large numbers'.

The Wagga Wagga post office was established on 1 January 1849, in charge of Frederick Anslow Tompson. Tompson, who was Clerk of Petty Sessions with a salary of £100 per annum, was actually a part-time postmaster. His postal allowance was £15 per annum.

It was a common practice to appoint the Clerk of Petty Sessions as postmaster at country towns. Postings were not heavy, and much of the mail was of an official nature . . .

It is reasonably certain that the first mails for Wagga Wagga were conveyed from the Port Phillip Road once a week via Tarcutta. A notice in the *Government Gazette* dated 1 August 1848 called for tenders for the carriage of mails on 'The Port Phillip Road' from and to Yass, Gundagai, Albury, Ovens, Seymour, Kilmore and Melbourne twice a week from 1 January 1849.

The rate of travelling required for the contractors was 'not less than six miles per hour, including all stoppages'. In 1856 the Tarcutta-Wagga service was increased to twice weekly and the following year a 'cross line' from Wagga Wagga to Deniliquin was established, 180 miles by horseback. The twice weekly mail was still being carried between Tarcutta and Wagga, a distance of 25 miles, in 1861, and during this year the 250-mile service by horseback from Wagga Wagga to Balranald was increased to once weekly.

There follow a number of details about the growth of the township ('by 1866 there were over 700 residents') and about public pressure for the enlargement of the post office premises because the landlord required the former office for his own use. There are notes, too, about floods 'a cause of great concern . . . one of the greatest having occurred in 1852' with a suggestion that the post office should be moved to a hill in the centre of the town, near the Court House, where it might be free from danger. Under such pioneering conditions special difficulties tended to arise. In 1878, after the Postmaster-General had agreed to the establishment of a separate post office and telegraph office the secretary of the Postal Reform Committee wrote:

Our town is a sort of halfway house between Sydney and Melbourne where travellers rest themselves for short periods and whence they despatch and receive letters and telegrams. Accustomed as these travellers are to the ample elbow room at the post offices in either metropolis, their astonishment at our want of accommodation would be amusing were it not vexatious.

They go to the post office for letters—find the sole window of communication closed, are jostled by an impatient and nearly always angry crowd, get wearied at the delay, and leave; or wait on until at length the window is opened when they find them-

selves shut out by the knowing ones who are aware of the difficulty, and hustled into an outer circle of women and children,
they listen to the sneers and scoffs hurled at the heads of the
post office clerks, who, goaded to indiscretion, not infrequently
retort in kind and evoke improper and unseemly scenes.

The official study, of which these extracts give only a brief outline, is contained in a 54-page booklet, with fascinating illustrations
taken from contemporary records. It is one of many such histories
prepared by the Historical Office of the Australian Postmaster-
General's Department. It is typical of the kind of research material
available to the collector who wishes to support his collection with
authentic background notes from official sources.

10
Exhibitions and Special Events

During the past 100 years or so many important functions of a local, national or international character have been postally honoured with commemorative cancellations covering an extraordinarily wide variety of activities. These have ranged from naval conferences and philatelic exhibitions to sanitary congresses, local flower shows, school anniversaries, high-level international gatherings, dog shows, Esperanto congresses, air displays and lawn tennis championships.

In England a pioneer of special event postmarks of this kind was the duplex-type circular date-stamp and killer bar in use between the period 5 May to 28 November 1862 at the International Exhibition, South Kensington, London, in connection with which a single-ring handstamp was also used for incoming mail.

London was again the venue for a number of exhibitions in the 1870s and 1880s. They included the Royal Agricultural Show of 1877, a similar exhibition in 1879, the Health Exhibition of 1884 and successively the Inventions Exhibition of 1885, the Colonial and Indian Exhibition of 1886 and the American Exhibition of June to October 1887.

All these occasions were honoured by a special postal imprint.

From this time forward exhibition and conference postmarks appeared to be granted status as a postal feature of many great foregatherings, not only in Britain but elswhere in the world.

The Penny Postage Jubilee of 1890, the Royal Naval Exhibition of 1891 and the Cork International Exhibition of 1902 were duly commemorated. In America the St Louis World Fair of 1904 and in New Zealand the Christchurch Exhibition of 1906 were productive of special date-stamps, as was the Franco-British Exhibition held in London in 1908, which was attended by more than 8,000,000 people. Across the Atlantic, in America and Canada special types of flag cancellations were used in 1899 to publicise the National Export Exposition and in 1901 to promote the Pan-American Exposition, the Canada Exposition in Toronto and the Provincial Exhibition in Victoria, BC.

In 1894 the great Agricultural Show of the Royal Agricultural Society of Great Britain took place at Cambridge. For this, and for succeeding shows at Reading, Bournemouth, Portsmouth and Wolverhampton special handstamps were in use. Sombre European war clouds overhung the International Exhibition at Bristol, England in 1914 and from that date, for several years, the issue of special handstamps declined in Great Britain.

However, in 1912 the first official Esperanto postmark was issued, in Austria. There followed from this source a special handstamp in 1913 for use in Switzerland, one for use in France in 1914, and at the end of hostilities one for use in Hungary in 1918. Two special Esperanto postmarks appeared in 1921 in Czechoslovakia, one in 1922 in Finland, three in Germany in 1923 and one in Austria in 1924.

As at December 1968 a total of 447 official Esperanto postmarks had been issued in 24 different countries in connection with congresses, inaugurations, exhibitions, anniversaries and other special events. Of this total Poland was the venue for 102 special handstamps, the rest were used in countries ranging from Argentina and Belgium to Japan, Cuba, Bulgaria and the Soviet Union. A full catalogue of Esperanto postmarks sponsored in connection with special events was published in Malmo, Sweden in 1965. The catalogue included illustrations of nine different specimens.

The British Empire Exhibition held at Wembley, England in 1924/5 brought about a great revival in this field and was productive of several distinctive types of postal impressions, including postal slogans used in other large centres of population to publicise the event and those used at the exhibition itself.

The interval of comparative peace between the two World Wars produced a wealth of absorbing material for the albums of the collector. In England, in 1926 special handstamps were used for agricultural shows at Bournemouth, Reading, Harrogate and Burnley and at philatelic congresses in Liverpool, and Nottingham. In 1928 a large double-ring handstamp was a feature of the London Stamp Exhibition.

Two years later representatives of most of the world's great naval powers gathered in London for a naval conference; in the same year, a sanitary congress at Margate, a philatelic congress in Devonshire, and a socialist Esperanto congress in Oxford were held. These meetings, otherwise unconnected, possessed from the viewpoint of the postmark collector one point of parallel interest: they were all considered to be of sufficient importance to merit the issue of special postal facilities and cancellation marks.

Thereafter the list is legion and virtually world wide. In 1932 the Swedish post office began using special first day postmarks for new issues, since when this country's special event postmarks have been a subject of growing interest. They have included, for example, a range of special handstamps honouring Swedish authors and poets and, in 1966, a circular handstamp to mark the occasion of the fifth World Congress on Fertility and Sterility, held in Stockholm in June that year.

India has been the source of postmarks commemorating such varied events as the All-India Radio Silver Jubilee Anniversary and the centenary anniversary in 1961 of the birth of Sir Rabindranath Tagore; a Malaria Eradication drive and an International Congress of Opthalmology in 1962; the Red Cross Centenary and a pioneer balloon mail flight at Bangalore in 1963 and an Indian Mount Everest Expedition in 1965.

Representing Scotland are exhibition handstamps of 1901 and 1908 and successive events thereafter on the lines of the Glasgow Empire Exhibition of 1938 and Royal Highland Shows at various venues.

The United States—to select three items from the wealth of material available—postally honoured the New York World's Fair of 1939, the Chicago Railroad Fair ten years later and the Lions International Stamp Club Congress, 1965.

In Berlin the occasion of the eleventh Olympiad of the Olympic Games produced a swastika-decorated memento and in Egypt in

1947 a bi-lingual cancellation marked the opening of the thirty-sixth Interparliamentary Union Conference. Complementary to these are the outpourings of France (International Aerial Post Exhibition, 1930); South Africa (National Philatelic Exhibition, Port Elizabeth, 1956); Switzerland (International Printing Exhibition, Lausanne, 1957); Belgium (the Brussels Fair, 1958); Italy (Medical Women's Congress, 1954); Germany (Leipzig Spring Fair, 1950); Canada (Provincial Exhibition, Victoria, BC, 1905); Papua and New Guinea (Rule of Law Seminar, Port Moresby, 1965); New Zealand (Methodist Missionary Anniversary, Kerikeri, 1972) and Australia (Australian Child Care Conference, Melbourne, 1972)—as well as innumerable other examples from these and other parts of the world.

In 1963 George R. Pearson, a founder member of the British Postmark Society, performed a useful service for the postmark collecting fraternity when he compiled and published an illustrated 52-page book on the subject of special event postmarks of the United Kingdom. This was the first real attempt to catalogue and describe the wide range of British postmarks—totalling well over 500 items—in this category. Valuations were given for many items and although these have long been surpassed they served at the time as a useful guide and the information has since been up-dated.

The publication of this book preceded a spectacular upsurge in the issue of special handstamps of pictorial or typeset design in Britain. In 1969, for example, the United Kingdom post office provided 250 special event handstamps, a figure exceeded in 1970 when 348 special event postmarks were released, obtainable for a face-value stamp expenditure of £5 16s, (£5·80). During 1971 a grand total of 280 special postmarks made their appearance in the United Kingdom. As a natural follow-up of this expanding interest the British Post Office announced in June 1971 the issue of a new fortnightly publication entitled *Postmark Bulletin* in which would be given full and reliable information about forthcoming releases of postmark slogans and special handstamps.

A separate collection of special event postmarks and those relating to international exhibitions, congresses and kindred occasions would recall and commemorate many memorable happenings. Thematically it would cover such subjects as sport, philately, religion and medicine. It would also be of considerable, and increasing, commercial value.

Here is a comparison of just 4 items listed and provisionally valued by Mr G. R. Pearson in his 1963 guide and the valuation (expressed in decimal currency) placed on similar items less than 5 years later:

	1963	1968
1894 Royal Show, Cambridge	£4	£12
1908 Edinburgh Exhibition	£1·50	£6
1911 Glasgow Exhibition	£2	£4·50
1911 Coronation Exhibition, London	£1·75	£5

The specialist in exhibition and kindred types of cancellations has an extensive and absorbing range from which to select material. It is an area in which the artwork and general standard of the handstamps themselves have tended to improve and become much more sophisticated and the events commemorated undoubtedly cover a very much wider sphere of human activity.

The collector now has at his disposal a field which fully rewards, in interest, variety and visual appeal, the long search which may sometimes precede the thrill of discovering a coveted specimen.

11
Slogans and Pictorial Cancellations

Soon after the dawn of the twentieth century the Canadian Post Office revived a centuries-old postal innovation, namely, the use of a form of postal slogan. One of these was in connection with an exposition at Toronto, the other was in support of a provincial exhibition at Victoria, BC. Both were in use in 1901.

In 1912 a similar type of Canadian postal message was introduced bearing the wording VANCOUVER MID-SUMMER FAIR AUG 10/17 1912. An earlier version, also used in Canada and loosely classifiable as a postal slogan, was a 'flag' type of cancellation (which itself made its debut at Boston, Massachusetts in 1894) used in 1897 to herald Queen Victoria's Diamond Jubilee. Most of the early Canadian flag cancels of this kind appeared in Toronto, but Victoria, British Columbia, also issued one incorporating numerals to represent the Jubilee dates with the name VICTORIA inserted.

Toronto followed this patriotic lead with another flag postmark in 1897, this time one which incorporated a Union Jack with a streamer bearing a shield containing the words CANADA'S EXPOSITION, TORONTO, AUGUST 26 TO SEPTEMBER 7.

From Bavaria in the autumn of 1910 came another pioneer slogan postmark, this time a pictorial machine cancellation which advertised the Oberammergau *Passionsspiele* (Passion Play). Specimens of this slogan, now relatively rare, can sometimes be found on picture post cards depicting the 'Kirche and Kofel' at Oberammergau.

The precedent for these enterprising moves lay deeply rooted in the fertile soil of post office initiative. More than 250 years

93

earlier, in 1661, correspondence passing through the Kent post in rural England had borne this quaintly-worded inscription:

The Post
For all Kent
Goes Every
Night From
The Round Ho-
-use in Love
Lane & Comes
Every Mor-
ninge

Another early version of a postmark slogan (a specimen was offered in auction in England for just over £11 in 1936 and would now be worth many times that amount) was the message impressed on correspondence despatched from St Osyth, Essex, in January 1674. It read: ESSEX POST GOES and COMS EVERY DAY. A variation of this slogan contains the letters SX in place of ESSEX.

After the Canadian revival little effective use was made of the postmark as a publicity medium until, in October 1917, outgoing mail from Boston, Massachusetts, was franked with a machine cancellation bearing the inscription BUY NOW US GOVERNMENT BONDS 2nd LIBERTY LOAN.

Among those who received and took note of the various messages conveyed by this economical and impressive means were officials of the British Post Office and also, apparently, those responsible for publicising Britain's own urgent fund-raising needs. In December 1917 the first of a series of three machine-franked slogans urging the British public to BUY NATIONAL WAR BONDS made its appearance. Unhappily a later version of the message, this time expressed in the form FEED THE GUNS WITH WAR BONDS, caused unforeseen embarrassment to British prisoners of war in German hands when letters from home bearing this somewhat provocative exhortation began to arrive in Germany.

Revived in the stress of war, the postal slogan had come to stay. Although its wartime use lapsed with the cessation of hostilities in 1918, a new popular use was found for it four years later—that of encouraging attendance at the 1922 British Industries Fair. In that year, also, the Republic of Ireland introduced its first postal slogan. It bore the somewhat enigmatic message LEARN IRISH TAILTEANN GAME AUGUST. The following year, in Canada, the Yorkton Stamp Exhibition was publicised by a slogan which is now in the hard-to-get category. Thereafter, in Britain, the ubiquitous slogan was put to equally effective use on behalf of the British Empire Exhibition, the Torchlight Tattoo at Wembley and—in 1926—to encourage employers of labour to JOIN THE KING'S ROLL AND EMPLOY WAR-DISABLED MEN.

Then followed a determined Post Office campaign to induce the British public to become telephone-minded. For several years internal mail bore such messages as SHOP BY TELEPHONE; GET THE TELEPHONE HABIT; TRADE FOLLOWS THE PHONE; THE TELEPHONE SAVES TIME AND MONEY and—an inspired variation of the same theme—YOU ARE WANTED ON THE PHONE.

Meanwhile early slogans and pictorial postmarks of diverse variety were making their appearance in other parts of the world.

In 1924 a curious Italian slogan used at Rome and Milan drew attention to the publication in the newspaper *Il Corriere Italiano* of 'MATA HARI a new romance by Guido da Verona'. Supporting this curious proclamation was a pictorial impression of the head and shoulders and scantily-clad upper half of the body of the unfortunate Dutch-born woman who posed as a Javanese and was shot as a spy at Vincennes, France in October 1917. Later, in the early 1930s, the first of an extensive and interesting range of Japanese circular pictorial postmarks made their appearance, soon to be followed by offerings from many other member-nations of the UPU.

From these beginnings has emerged a long and apparently unending stream of postal slogans and commercial mail meter marks and pictorial slogans, the collection and study of which provides unbounded opportunities for collectors in all parts of the world.

Inevitably, some amusing and occasionally embarrassing results have derived from such a vast outpouring of postal slogans. One early airmail flight carried letters franked IT'S QUICKER TO TELEGRAPH—in its context, a tactless comment. On another occasion, in Ireland, publicity used at Carlow for a rural week promotion was supported by a postal slogan which gave the wrong dates for the event. Elsewhere in the world it is recorded that subscriber telephone accounts were on one occasion dispatched in envelopes bearing the postal inscription A STILL TONGUE MAKES A GOOD CITIZEN.

There have been complaints—vociferously expressed in some sections of the British Press—that slogans used on picture post-cards tend partly to obliterate the senders' messages. In reply to one such complaint a head postmaster wrote: 'We do ask our customers to leave a clear margin above the address of not less than $1\frac{1}{2}$ in (4 cm) deep for the postage stamps and postmarks. The margin should extend across the whole width of the correspondence and address panels of a picture postcard.'

That did not prevent one person from pointing out that the purpose of writing cards was to convey a message to the recipient and that advertisement franking could be confined to the more suitable expanse of envelopes and parcels.

There have been other classic cases of the unfortunate and often unforeseen effects of postal slogans. One woman received a notice from her local hospital to go for a minor operation. Across the envelope was franked the sinister message ARE YOU FULLY INSURED? In Eastbourne (Sussex) and Bridlington (Yorkshire) recipients of court summonses for alleged violations of traffic regulations received envelopes respectively marked YOU'LL COME TO LOVE EASTBOURNE and SEE YOU AT BRIDLINGTON.

The World Refugee slogan postmark of 1960—the pictorial element of which, a hand raised in supplication, was designed by the eminent artist Dame Laura Knight—had equally repercussive effects when it was found that in juxtaposition with the contemporary British postage stamps the thumb of the upraised hand often fell neatly in line with the British queen's nose.

In 1966 a headmaster received by post from Edinburgh an issue of the National Savings Movement newsletter in a wrapper on which the Post Office had franked the slogan COME RACING AT MUSSELBURGH. During the same year an eminent churchman launched a diocesan movement urging people to rethink their faith. To publicise this a small sticker worded 'Opportunity Unlimited' was fixed to outgoing correspondence. Unhappily this

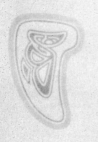

FIRST DAY COVER

TAGORE CENTENARY

7 MAY 1961

INDIAN POSTS & TELEGRAPHS

R.K.Forster
122 Scholes Park Road
Scarborough, England.

worthy message was counterbalanced by a postal slogan which bore the words YORK RACES, MAY 18, 19, 20.

Hardly less inopportune was the juxtaposition, in Canada in 1957, of a series of four postage stamps emphasising the delights of outdoor sports, including hunting and fishing, the issue of which coincided with the use of a postal slogan which said CONSERVE CANADA'S WILDLIFE.

Indeed, Canada's postal messages, although no doubt clear and explicit in their country of origin, often puzzle overseas recipients. The enigmatic phrase WHY WAIT FOR SPRING ? DO IT NOW! is a case in point. The idea of the slogan is admirable: many Canadian businesses are busy in summer and slack during the winter months. Thus, home-owners who require a job doing are encouraged to give the work to someone in the winter and so help to provide year-round employment. But in countries less concerned with such climatic considerations the purpose of the message was far from clear. More explicit, but in its way equally intriguing is the sporting communication conveyed in the Nelson, BC, cancellation of the 1960s: CURLING AMID THE ROSES—SUMMER BONSPIEL, JULY 4–9, 1966.

On the other hand, the Canadian slogan CANADIAN STAMPS ARE NECESSARY ON MAIL POSTED IN CANADA appears on the face of it to be stating the obvious. But in fact the message, also used on mail boxes at airports and border points, is intended as a tactful reminder to foreign visitors, especially those from the United States, who have been known to use foreign stamps on letters posted in the Dominion.

Another Canadian slogan, used in 1971, carries the wording AVOID THE XMAS BLUSH, followed by the words VOTRE AFFAIRE EST DANS LE SAC SI VOUS POSTEZ TÔT. Here again, the message presumably makes good sense in Toronto, Montreal and Winnipeg which, as far as the Canadian Post Office is concerned, is the principal object of the exercise.

Conversely, such British postal slogans as HUDDERSFIELD RAG WEEK and YOU DIG HARLOW, WHY NOT DIG AN ALLOTMENT ? might be equally puzzling to a Canadian addressee.

As in Britain, the American postal authorities exercise a responsible degree of supervision on the subject of postal slogans.

Many apparently innocuous phrases have been firmly turned down in both countries because of the possibility of some almost undetectable slight to a sensitive section of the public. The rules cover anything obscene, liable to advocate treason or insurrection, or likely to libel, threaten or offend a specific group or individual. Indeed, the slogan REPORT OBSCENE MAIL TO YOUR POSTMASTER has itself been used on American mail and a close watch is kept for possible contraventions of the regulations.

Nonetheless, both in Britain and America, there have been occasional instances where the borderline case—the controversial or the frankly unacceptable slogan—has managed to slip past officialdom's watchful eye.

When the slogan THE BEST INVESTMENT A TELEPHONE was used in Britain in 1936 the left-hand corner of a section of the slogan's frame was mistaken by some people for an 'L' making part of the message appear to be LA TELEPHONE. Several irate people wrote to their newspapers complaining about the use of a French word on British postmarks, although in more recent years French phrases have been used without comment. Equally unacceptable to one recipient was the British road safety slogan REMEMBER THAT ROAD ACCIDENTS ARE CAUSED BY PEOPLE LIKE YOU. An indignant naval officer looked upon the stricture as a personal indictment of his driving ability and made strong protest through legal channels.

American mail bearing the meter slogan HELP STAMP OUT HUMAN BEINGS was also reported in 1963 to have been the subject of comment. And the receipt by some worthy citizens of mail bearing Statue of Liberty postage stamps and the proud inscription 'Liberty For All' was tinged in the eyes of some recipients with an element of satire by the overprinted slogan ALIENS MUST REPORT THEIR ADDRESSES DURING JANUARY.

Within this category a classic of its kind was the drought period British postal slogan PLEASE USE LESS WATER which happened, unfortunately, to be overprinted on mail sent out to a London brewery. Two other British slogans which produced sharp reaction were the 1949 message BRITAIN SAYS THANK YOU FOR FOOD GIFTS and, nearly 20 years later, the use of SHIP THROUGH NEWPORT (MON.) THE HOME OF THE MOLE WRENCH. Objection to the first of these was on the grounds (to quote one indignant Press letter-writer) that this mendicant phrase 'took the form of begging from our neighbours'. Disapproval of the second slogan was based on the precept that no private advertising should appear on postmarks applied by the Post Office—the Mole Wrench being, in fact, a multi-purpose hand tool produced by a Newport engineering firm.

During the 15 months of its existence the MOLE WRENCH slogan—brainchild of Mrs T. R. Coughtrie, wife of the engineering firm's managing director—appeared on something like 15 million items of mail for a total outlay of about £100. It was also accorded third place in a Sunday newspaper's nationwide competition designed to find the most memorable advertisement of 1968.

However, following objections to its use, the Mole Wrench version of the slogan was formally withdrawn on 31 March 1969 and replaced by one with different phrasing: SHIP THROUGH NEWPORT (MON) THE HOME OF THE SELF-GRIP WRENCH.

The incident had an interesting, if not quite parallel, precedent. In the summer of 1926 the British Postmaster-General, Sir William Mitchell-Thomson, announced a plan to incorporate commercial advertisements in the slogan section of machine cancellations. Several firms opposed the idea on the grounds that they did not wish their outgoing mail to carry the advertisements of their competitors. The Halifax (Yorkshire) confectionery manufacturing firm John Mackintosh and Sons felt so strongly about this that they produced a special envelope with a black band along the top, designed to render ineffective any slogan printed across it. The border area of the envelope carried the firm's own clearly printed riposte: NEVER MIND THE POSTMARK—THIS IS THE RIGHT TIME TO BUY MACKINTOSH'S TOFFEE de LUXE.

This bold and defiant measure drew a strong response from officialdom. The firm was formally instructed to stop using its overprinted envelopes. But the battle was not yet over. Mackintosh's questioned the right of the Post Office to deface the envelopes of a private firm with advertisements in favour of rival products and after the matter had been raised in the British House of Commons the Post Office proposal was discreetly abandoned.

An interesting postscript to this polite but bitterly fought battle between the Post Office and private enterprise was the appearance on 5 May 1972 of a special handstamp to commemorate the official opening of the Post House (Hotel), Stockton-on-Tees, Teesside, England. Neatly tucked in the lower corner of this officially-applied postal marking was a widely-known and recognised symbol representing the trading sign and initials of a well-known catering and hotel-owning group!

Until 1963 slogan postmarks in Britain were used only for government-sponsored campaigns, including publicity for national and local events. Then the rules were relaxed to allow local authorities to sponsor tourist and prestige postmarks. Britain's first pictorial postmark in this category was also one of the most happily inspired.

It was put into use at Hastings in April 1963 and featured Happy Harold, the cheerful warrior, ready for a holiday invasion under the caption WE'RE READY FOR YOUR INVASION AT HASTINGS— an enterprising tie-up with the historically famous battle of Senlac Hill in 1066. Civic recognition of the use of this slogan was provided by the presence of the Mayor of Hastings who inaugurated the use of the new postmark dies. As an inspired follow-up to this pioneer tourist slogan Hastings later used the equally famous catchline POPULAR WITH VISITORS SINCE 1066.

From that modest beginning the use of tourist and prestige postmark slogans has spread throughout Britain. In 1963 there were 104 campaigns, followed by 196 in 1964, 230 in 1965, 240 in 1966 and 339 in 1967. One reason for their undoubted success and popularity has been the inexpensive means they provide for placing thousands of advertisements in homes, shops and offices.

By this medium, over the years, Britons have been enjoined to LEARN TO SWIM; LEND A HAND ON THE LAND; KEEP DEATH OFF THE ROAD; TAKE STAGGERED HOLIDAYS FOR COMFORT; FLY BY BRITISH AIRLINES and, with the hurried impartiality of machines franking between 300 and 900 letters a minute, to DIG FOR VICTORY and PICK AN ENGLISH COX—the last being a reference to a type of dessert apple originated in 1825 in the garden of Mr Cox, a retired brewer.

Other countries have adopted the idea with perhaps even greater versatility. In addition to such conventional examples as FIJI

OFFERS FUN IN THE SUN; TEACH YOUR CHILDREN TO CLEAN THEIR
TEETH; PREVENT BUSH FIRES and USE AUSTRALIAN PRODUCTS there
can be found a large number of pictorial and text-type slogans
from many world areas, including Switzerland, Denmark, France,
Belgium and the Netherlands in which skilled artwork has attract-
ively added to the overall effectiveness of the postal slogan's
message.

Here to indicate the range, is a selection of assorted slogans
from various parts of the world during the past 40 years:

OBESITY SHORTENS LIFE TREAT IT SERIOUSLY
(Guernsey, Channel Islands, 1970)
THE RIDDLE OF ZIMBABWE
(Southern Rhodesia, 1958)
PUT CHRIST BACK INTO CHRISTMAS
(Edmonton, Alberta, Canada, 1955)
THINK OF THE OLD AT CHRISTMAS
(Leeds, England, 1961)
SUPPORT RED FEATHER
(Sarnia, Ontario, 1966)
MAKE FRIENDS WITH A DEAF CHILD
(Northampton, England, 1971)
CONQUER CYSTIC FIBROSIS
(Las Vegas, Nevada, USA, 1966)
DIPHTHERIA!! IS YOUR CHILD IMMUNISED?
(Dublin, Ireland, 1952)
BECKER JUNIOR COLLEGE 75th ANNIVERSARY, 1887–1962
(Worcester, Massachusetts, USA, 1962)
THE SAFE CIGARETTE IS THE ONE YOU DON'T LIGHT
(Victoria, BC, Canada, 1968)
PRÉSERVEZ VOS YEUX, ECLAIREZ VOUS MIEUX
(Paris, France, 1969)
PRAY FOR PEACE
(Mansfield, Ohio, USA, 1957)
COME TO SUNNY MALTA THE ISLAND OF HISTORY AND ROMANCE
(Valletta, Malta, 1926)
LEPROSY CAN BE STOPPED WITH MODERN DRUG TREATMENT
(Ndola, Zambia, 1969)

SEND GOOD NEWS TELEGRAMS
(Johannesburg, South Africa, 1937)
FIND A BIN PUT IT IN—KEEP HARLOW TIDY
(Harlow, Essex, England, 1970)
HELP STAMP OUT SMUGGLING
(Manila, Philippines)
WATER MEANS LIFE
(East London, South Africa, 1970)
DON'T DISCUSS TROOP MOVEMENTS!
(Sydney, Australia, 1942)
PIU' VELOCITA PIU' PERICOLO
(Milan, Italy, 1968)
SANE DRIVING SAFE ARRIVING
(Innisfail, Australia, 1962)
IS DEATH A PASSENGER IN YOUR CAR?
(Zambia, 1971)
SPEND YOUR VACATION IN SUMMERLAND
(Kingston, Jamaica, 1936)
NORWAY—LAND OF THE MIDNIGHT SUN
(Oslo, Norway, 1960)
WHAT RHODESIA MAKES, MAKES RHODESIA
(Causeway, Southern Rhodesia, 1960)
OLD MEDICINES CAN KILL—DESTROY UNUSED MEDICINES
(St Albans, England, 1970)
SALES ABROAD MAKE JOBS AT HOME
(Chicago, Illinois, USA, 1960)
EAT APPLES FOR HEALTH
(Toronto, Canada, 1940)
GIBRALTAR THE TRAVEL KEY OF THE MEDITERRANEAN
(Gibraltar, 1932)
LUTON HATS HEAD THE WORLD
(Luton, England, 1967)
BE FRIENDLY AND COURTEOUS TO TOURISTS
(Regina, Saskatchewan, Canada, 1950)
REMEMBER TO DIP
(Dublin, Ireland, 1970)
WHEREVER YOU GO THERE'S RADIO
(Sydney, Australia, 1961)

Slogans and Pictorial Cancellations

REMEMBER ONLY YOU CAN PREVENT FOREST FIRES
(Boston, Massachusetts, USA, 1965)
PAY NO MORE THAN CEILING PRICES
(Ottawa, Canada, 1945)
ELECTRICITY MAKES MISHAPS RARE
(Brisbane, Australia, 1961)
TREASURES OF TUTANKHAMUN AT THE BRITISH MUSEUM
(London, England, 1972)
BLACK MARKET DEALINGS WEAKEN THE COMMUNITY
(Zurich, Switzerland, 1942)
CORRECT ADDRESSING IS A BLESSING, SAVES US GUESSING
(St John's, Antigua, 1970)
PARCHWYCH EIN CEFN GWLAD—PLEASE RESPECT
    OUR COUNTRYSIDE
(Bangor, Wales, 1969)
HELP TO WIN ON THE KITCHEN FRONT
(London, England, 1940)
CANCER CAN BE BEATEN
(Medicine Hat, Alberta, Canada, 1969)
OBSERVEZ LA JOURNÉE DE LA FAIM
(Geneva, Switzerland, 1962)
SHIP VIA DOVER THE SHORT SEA ROUTE
(Dover, England, 1972)
THE AGENCY WITH A HEART—USC'S 25th YEAR—OTTAWA
(Vancouver, Canada, 1969)
KEEP NEW ZEALAND GREEN—PREVENT FOREST FIRES
(Christchurch, New Zealand, 1953)
YOUR ONE GIFT WORKS MANY WONDERS
(Don Mills, Ontario, Canada, 1966)
OBSERVE SUNDAY
(Vancouver, BC, Canada, 1946)
BUON NATALE, BUON ANNO
(Florence, Italy, 1968)
THE PANAMA CANAL—SHORT ROUTE TO WORLD MARKETS
(Cristobal, Canal Zone, 1956)
COME TO THE BOYS AND GIRLS FAIR
(Edmonton, Alberta, Canada, 1950)
SPONSOR A BRITISH MIGRANT

(Perth, Western Australia, 1959)
CONSERVE COAL—SAVE ONE TON IN FIVE
(Calgary, Alberta, Canada, 1943)
DON'T WASTE BREAD OTHERS NEED IT
(Wakefield, England, 1946)
GIVE CHILDREN HEALTH—USE HEALTH STAMPS
(Wellington, New Zealand, 1968)
WITHOUT A NEWSPAPER YOU LIVE ON THE MOON
(Danzig, 1938)

By means of the postal slogan Mexico has proclaimed the evils of alcoholism and Trinidad the virtues of its sugar. Canadian cancels have said that CANADA'S DOORS ARE OPEN TO TOURISTS; New Zealand in 1940 has uttered the all-embracing exhortation: DON'T WASTE ANYTHING USEFUL, and the voice of the geographically remote Shetland Isles has been heard postally to proclaim NOWHERE ELSE IN THE WORLD WILL YOU FIND SUCH FINE WOOL KNITTED SO SKILFULLY, LOVINGLY, PATIENTLY, AS IN THE SHETLAND ISLES. Traffic dangers and trade fairs, black market activities, smuggling, oral hygiene, community anniversaries and noisy radios have all at various times been appropriately commended or condemned by this versatile postal medium.

The collection of postal slogans and pictorial postmarks provides a fascinating opportunity to study the sociological, historical and political background of many nations during many decades. Moreover, the story behind each individual slogan (its origin, artwork, source, dates of use and underlying purpose) almost always rewards the researcher.

Material is not difficult to come by and it can be arranged either in chronological, geographical or thematic sequence without the use of expensive albums. Cut into strips the slogans can be mounted on sheets in a loose-leaf album or on plain sheets housed in a box-file. Accumulated and maintained in this way the world's steady stream of postal persuasion and propaganda holds attractive possibilities for the specialist collector.

12
Collecting by Theme

Philatelists frequently collect not only by country but by topic or theme. Doctors, for example, may be attracted to postage stamps depicting medical treatment, hospitals and healing; the student of heraldry may be tempted to look for issues bearing armorial designs, crests and badges; the connoisseur of art might concentrate on specimens portraying famous artists and their works; the naturalist might be drawn to material linked with botany or zoology and the man with a military background might look for stamps dealing with weapons, equipment, campaigns and battles.

For the cancellations collector opportunities no less varied are offered. All the themes mentioned, and a great many more, are available. With the exercise of a little patience and ingenuity groups of postmarks can be gathered on almost every subject from animals and birds to beverages and bridges and a basic collection begun in this way can soon be enlarged with the co-operation of friends and fellow collectors.

With postmarks, the subject can be expressed either by the pictorial content of the design (as in the case of special handstamps, for instance) or by means of a link which can be provided by the postal place-name or some kindred association. Thus, a special handstamp depicting a type of scientific microscope or a new hospital building might be eligible for inclusion in a collection of medical postmarks on the basis of its pictorial content, whereas one from a health exhibition or a place named Hygiene or Helix might be acceptable because of a medical link with its place of origin.

Perhaps the best way to indicate the manner in which a really large and interesting collection can be developed along these lines,

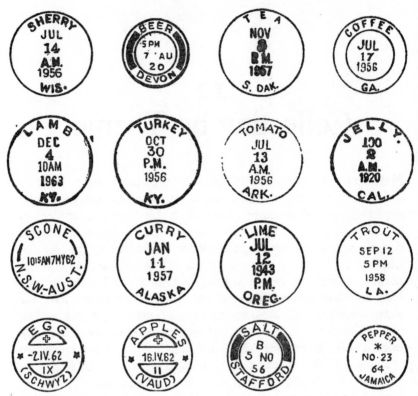

9 *Food and drink*

with a theme as its basis, would be to take two or three practical examples and deal with them in outline, and then follow this in a succeeding chapter with an example of a theme developed in more detail.

For a start, hotel postmarks offer a wide-ranging and exciting challenge to the collector of unusual items. Comparatively few of the world's well-known hotels can boast a postmark bearing their name, and many that could formerly do so are no longer in existence. The search for bygone rarities and for postal markings still current and available is well worth the trouble. It spans oceans and continents and can produce rewards from many unexpected places.

Here is a specimen check-list of some of the world's hotels which have at one time or another possessed on-the-spot post office facilities or a distinctive official postmark bearing their own name:

Australia: Mayne Hotel (Queensland); Meadows Hotel (New South Wales); Palace Hotel (Perth, Western Australia); Quondong Hotel (New South Wales).

Austria: Hotel Defreggerhof; Semmering Hotel; Sulden Hotel.

Belgium: Hotel Albert I (Brussels).

Canada: Banff Springs Hotel (Alberta).

Egypt: Cataract Hotel (Aswan); Continental Savoy Hotel (Cairo); Ghesireh Palace Hotel (Cairo); Grand Continental Hotel (Cairo); Heliopolis Palace Hotel (Heliopolis); Luxor Hotel (Luxor); San Stefano Hotel (Ramleh); Savoy Hotel (Cairo); Shepheard's Hotel (Cairo); Winter Palace Hotel (Luqsor).

England: Grand Hotel (Scarborough, Yorkshire); Grand Hotel Building (Eastbourne, Sussex); Hilton Hotel (London); Hotel Cecil (London); Langham Hotel (London); Midland Hotel (Manchester, Lancashire).

France: Grand Hôtel (Paris); Hôtel-de-Ville (Limoges, Haute Vienne).

India: Burlington Hotel (Lucknow); Carlton Hotel (Lucknow); Charleville Hotel (Mussooree); Grand Hotel (Calcutta); Great Eastern Hotel (Calcutta); Hotel Republic (Patna); Maiden's Hotel (Delhi); Metropole (Agra); Mussooree Savoy Hotel, (Dehra Dun); Oberoi Palace Hotel, (Srinagar); Royal Hotel (Meerut); Wild Flower Hotel (Simla).

Italy: Albergo di Russia (Rome); Albergo Dolomiti (Belluno); Albergo Esperia (Rome); Albergo Flora (Rome); Albergo Loreto (Milan); Albergo Molveno (Molveno-Trento); Albergo Palazzo degli Ambasciatori (Rome); Albergo Plaza (Rome); Albergo Solda (Bolzano); Albergo Terminus (Naples); Albergo Touring (Milan); Albergo val Martello (Bolzano); Alpino Strese Grand Hotel (Novara); Grand Hôtel des Bains (Venice); Grand Hotel (Milan);

Grand Hotel Villa d'Este (Cernobbio); Hotel Bristol (Rome); Hotel Excelsior Italia (Florence); Hotel Grand Bretagne (Florence); Hotel Milano (Rome); Hotel Pordoi (Trento); Hotel Principe e Savoia (Milan); Hotel Quirinale (Rome); Modern Hotel (Rome).

Jamaica: Constant Spring Hotel.

Japan: Hotel New Japan (Akasaka, Tokyo); Hotel Okura-Nai (Akasaka, Tokyo); Keikoku Hotel (Tokyo); Tokyo Hotel (Tokyo); Imperial Hotel (Tokyo); New Otani Hotel (Tokyo).

Mexico: Hotel del Palmar (Veracruz); Hotel Hacienda Uxmal (Yucatan).

Netherlands Antilles: Aruba Caribbean Hotel (Aruba)

Pakistan: Beach Luxury Hotel (Karachi); Dean's Hotel (Peshawar); Faletti's Hotel (Lahore); Hotel Metropole (Karachi); Hotel Shambagh (Dacca, now geographically Bangladesh).

Penang: Eastern and Oriental Hotel; Runnymede Hotel.

Philippines: Manila Hotel (Manila)

Scotland: Gleneagles Hotel (Perthshire); Hydropathic (Peebles); Hydropathic (Crieff, Perthshire); Lochboisdale Hotel (Isle of S Uist); The Marine Hotel (East Lothian).

Singapore: Raffles Hotel; Sea View Hotel.

Thailand: Erewan Hotel (Bangkok); Rama Hotel (Bangkok); Royal Hotel (Bangkok).

United States of America: Hotel Champlain (New York); Curtis Hotel (Minneapolis).

There are, in addition, a number of postmarks marginally admissible on this theme in the sense that the post offices from which they derive are actually located in hotel premises, although the wording of the postmark may not disclose this fact.

To inquire into the background of postmark sources such as

those appearing in the foregoing list can prove to be most rewarding.

Let us take a specific example:

Using 35 architects and an army of men working day and night, the 17-storey 1100-bedroom Hotel New Otani in Tokyo, Japan, was built in 15 months in preparation for the 1964 Olympic Games. The hotel stands in 15 acres of traditionally styled Japanese gardens. Its facilities include 13 restaurants and, on the seventeenth floor, a superbly-styled revolving Blue Sky cocktail lounge which seats 350 people and does one complete revolution every hour giving an extensive panorama of the city. The hotel possesses full post office facilities and outgoing mail is date-stamped with an official postmark worded 'Hotel New Otani, Tokyo, Japan'.

A collection of entirely different calibre could be gathered under the heading 'Borderline Postmarks'. Such a collection would include odd spots on the map where erratic man-made boundaries may cause brothers to serve in different armies or men to sleep with their feet in one country and their heads in another. As a thematic field this is an exciting one to explore for it touches many out of the way places with on-the-brink links.

Hungerford, Australia, is an interesting point at which to begin. Its post office opened—as Hungerford's—in New South Wales on 1 January 1876. On 1 October 1880 the office was officially transferred to the state of Queensland. One year later, to the day, it did a kangaroo hop—metaphorically speaking—back into New South Wales.

Referring, in 1966, to this remarkable sequence a contemporary writer said 'its pub is in Queensland and its post office is in New South Wales'. But in February 1967 postmaster D. E. Watt answered the present writer's inquiry by stating emphatically 'Hungerford is in Queensland'—an assertion borne out by the postmark on his letter. He added: 'Years ago I believe the office was in New South Wales, approximately 300 yards from the site of the existing office. A 6-foot high netting fence now runs along the border between New South Wales and Queensland.'

Occasionally the name of a place suggests its borderline character. Mexicali sits on one side of the Mexico-California stateline; Calexico lies on the other. Monida, a beef-ranching town in Montana, USA, takes its name from Montana and Idaho upon whose boundaries it lies. Bordertown, South Australia, named when the borderline was in dispute, lies 11·4 miles (18·4 km) from the Victoria boundary; Border, a village in Cape Province, South Africa straddles the frontier with the neighbouring province of Orange Free State; Frontier, in Lincoln County, Wyoming, USA, was named in 1897 for its proximity to the Utah-Wyoming stateline and State Line, a Mississippi postal place-name, denotes the meeting point of Mississippi and Alabama.

Further north, the town of Marydel links Maryland and Delaware (with commendable impartiality its post office delivers mail to patrons in both states) and Armorel derives from the abbreviated forms of Arkansas and Missouri linked with the letters REL—the initials of a man named Wilson who is said to have founded this sawmill town.

Illmo has an obvious affinity with Illinois and Missouri; Arkoma unites Arkansas and Oklahoma and in Canada Alsask sits astride the boundary between the provinces of Alberta and Saskatchewan. Texarkana, another borderline case, unites in its postmark the names of Texas, Arkansas and Louisiana.

In Australia, on 11 June 1969, a special 38 mm rubber postmarker handstamp was used to mark the unveiling of a plaque at a point where the boundaries of New South Wales, Queensland and South Australia meet, thus commemorating the work of surveyor John Cameron who was responsible for fixing the boundaries in 1880.

Sometimes the borderline is that of a county rather than a state or province. Inyokern, California—earlier known as Magnolia—adopted its present name in 1913 because it lies near the boundaries of Inyo and Kern counties and Colmor, New Mexico, whose post office was founded in 1887, adopted the name from the first three letters in the names of Colfax and Mora counties whose edges the town touches.

In 1951 the Universal Postal Union correctly located the European town of Elten, Netherlands, in the province of Gelderland. The next edition of the Union's register allocated the town to the German postal region of Düsseldorf. A press report dated 2 August 1963 explains why: 'The 3,600 inhabitants of Elten went to bed last night in Holland and woke up today in West Germany. The reason is that Elten, plus about 15,800 acres of Dutch-German border country, was handed back by the Dutch Government to West Germany at midnight. The area was given to Holland after the Second World War, pending a peace treaty with Germany. A Dutch-German treaty was signed at The Hague in April 1960.'

Thus, behind two postmarks deriving from the same point of mailing lies a human story of how, overnight, at the stroke of a pen, several thousand citizens changed their nationality, no doubt in many instances with consequent upheaval in their private lives.

Further afield, in South America, the village of Valle California—formerly in Argentina—also changed hands and became part of Chile. Underlying the transfer, which now causes the community's postmark to read 'Valle California, Correos, Chile', is an interesting sidelight on an aspect of international diplomacy which only recently came to an end.

Chile has a very long boundary with Argentina, most of it mountainous and sparsely inhabited. It is understandable that differences of opinion as to exactly where the frontier runs should have arisen from time to time and in 1902 a general treaty on the subject of arbitration gave the neighbouring countries the right to call on the British Government to arbitrate on doubtful points that could not be resolved by direct negotiation. It was signed at a time when British influence in the region was strong and it was automatically renewed every ten years if neither Chile nor Argentina asked for it to be revoked.

At the beginning of 1972 Argentina suggested that the idea of a third country deciding disputes between neighbours had become outdated and pointed out that the International Court at The Hague provided adequate machinery for settling such points of difference. Chile agreed. A new treaty was signed, making the Court the new referee. The postmark of Valle California thus commemorates one of the last occasions when the system of British arbitration was employed in this region.

Almost every part of the world can contribute interesting material towards a collection of borderline postmarks (see figure 8).

In Kenya the date-stamp of Equator, a meteorological station straddling the earth's bulging waistline, would be admissible; in the Fiji islands the handstamp of Waiyevo also has a claim to inclusion: the 180° meridian slices through the town's main street, dividing East from West and yesterday from today, a geographical oddity commemorated by the issue of a special postmark.

Borderline anomalies of another kind arise in Britain where a familiar place such as Gretna Green, geographically in Dumfriesshire, Scotland, and romantically linked with the theme of runaway marriages, has been arbitrarily assigned for purposes of postal administration to Carlisle, Cumberland, England. Similarly, Woodville—an English town once known by the extraordinary name Wooden Box—is postally in the county of Staffordshire and geographically in the counties of Derbyshire and Leicestershire.

Enclave communities and their postmarks provide a particularly interesting sidelight on the labyrinthine complexities of human affairs. The town of Baarle-Hertog, for example, comprises a Belgian enclave in Dutch territory. A Belgian possession since 1479, the town was divided between North Brabant (now a Dutch province) and South Brabant (Belgian territory) in such a singular fashion that the market place is Dutch, except for one tavern, and the old church is Belgian. In one cafe the billiards table intersects the frontier so that the balls make short international journeys as the game proceeds.

Baarle-Hertog's unique situation preserved it from the German occupation during the First World War and it became an important centre of Allied espionage. Its status as an enclave was confirmed by the Belgian-Netherlands treaty of separation in 1839 and the town's double-ring handstamp, worded 'Baarle-Hertog, Belgische Enclaves in Nederland' symbolises its curious situation in the complicated world of borderline communities.

Llivia, Spain, is a town with kindred problems. It occupies a part of Gerona province, Spain, which consists of an enclave of 5 square miles (13 sq. km) in the Pyrénées-Orientales department of France, 4 miles (6 km) north-east of Puigcerda, Spain. Grazing, subsistence agriculture and smuggling have been quoted as its principle sources of livelihood. Its postmark reads 'Llivia, Gerona, Espana'. This curious enclosure resulted from the Pyrenees peace treaty of 1659 which accidentally excluded Llivia from a list of border villages assigned to France.

XII Post office, Wellington Hospital, New Zealand

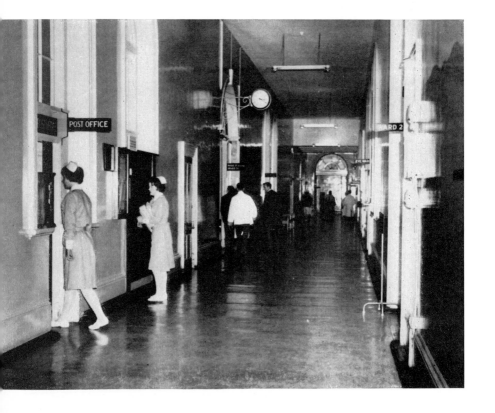

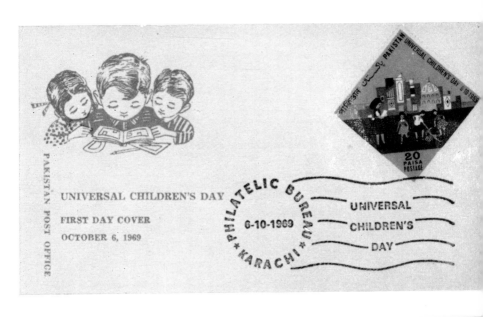

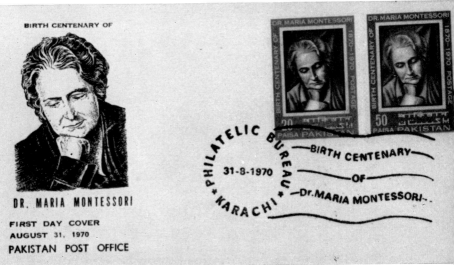

10 Postmarks from high places

These examples reveal, perhaps, something of the potential scope of a postmark collection related to a thematic subject, the opportunities for which are virtually without limit.

The theme of 'High Places' is one from which the collector could gain much pleasure and interest. A gathering of material on this subject could include the postmarks of Table Mountain (Cape Town, South Africa); Mount Ruapehu (New Zealand); Ayers Rock (Northern Territory, Australia) and the Indian Mount Everest Expedition of 1965. To these one could add the postmarks of Cerro de Pasco, Peru—at 14, 385 feet (4,359 m) reputedly the highest permanent post office in the world—or that of Climax, Colorado (11,320 feet or 3,430 m) claimed in 1955 to be 'the highest post office in the United States of those which are open all the year round'. Many other high towns and mountaineering mementoes could be postally represented in such a collection. Cabramurra, New South Wales, 4,880 feet (1,455 m) above sea level is said to be the highest town in Australia, and Namche Bazar, Nepal, is claimed to be the nearest permanent post office to Everest.

Nor is this lofty theme limited to earthbound heights of Man's endeavours and achievements. When the first lunar post office was established, with minimal equipment, by the crew of the Apollo II moonlanding project in 1969 an historic memento of the event was a special single-circle cancellation bearing the words MOON LANDING, USA and the date JUL 20 1969.

Other items which the collector could successfully pursue include banking, insurance, aviation, literary postmarks, island postmarks, men (and women) on the map, postmarks and royalty, ships and the sea, postmarks classified by type, ghost towns, disaster date-stamps, history, the law, railway postmarks, travelling post offices and an immense range of themes linked with such subjects as music, the arts, motoring, religion, education and sport.

To indicate how a typical check-list can be compiled with one specific subject in mind is the object of the next chapter.

Christmas postmarks

13
Focus on a Theme

In this section an attempt has been made to develop in closer detail the preparation of a check list of postmarks available on a single theme; in this example that of medicine, health and healing.

Long before the nature of contagion was understood it was common practice in some parts of the world to disinfect items of mail as a precaution against the spread of disease. There is evidence to suggest that as early as the fourteenth century measures were being taken—at Ragusa on the Adriatic coast for example—to disinfect sea-borne mail and by the mid-fifteenth century the practice is known to have been followed in Venice. Britain, late in the field, did not take up the idea until 1637.

Items thus treated, by immersion in vinegar or sea-water, or merely by piercing the item to fumigate it and allow 'noxious odours' to escape, were sometimes indicated by the addition of distinctive handstamps or seals or manuscript annotations usually applied by health authorities. In this way and for this reason an historic link was forged between postal markings and the basic precepts of preventive medicine, although modern authorities ascribe from the health viewpoint few benefits, if any, to the elaborate measures taken. The link thus established has been immeasureably strengthened and increased in the intervening centuries.

Since those early days a mass of postmarks of many kinds has proliferated from world-wide sources to make the compiling of a medical postmarks collection an absorbing and compelling study. To begin with, there are in Australia alone—to select a specimen region—at least 100 places which owe their names to medical men. A specific survey on this subject carried out by Professor J. B.

Cleland of the University of Adelaide and published in 1934 in *The Medical Journal of Australia* developed this area of research in a fascinating way.

It revealed, for instance, that in New South Wales alone 21 medical men have given their names to 25 places. In Western Australia the names of 28 men of medicine have been similarly honoured in 32 different places.

In addition there are hundreds of hospital and sanatorium post offices all over the world which frank outgoing mail with their own postmark impressions. There are many others where the link is less apparent. One can experience a pioneering sense of research and discovery by bringing to light the relevance of postmarks such as those from Coxsackie (New York State), Redfern (New South Wales) or Helix (Oregon) to this theme.

Let us pursue these three examples and see where they lead us. Coxsackie, in Greene County, New York State—near the west bank of the Hudson River—is eligible as a medical postmark because the town has the dubious distinction of having bequeathed its name to that of a virus. The town was settled by the Dutch before 1700 and incorporated in 1867. Of the link between the town and the virus that bears its name one standard medical dictionary has this to say: 'Coxsackie viruses are a group of viruses so called because they were first isolated from two patients with a disease resembling paralytic poliomyelitis in the village of Coxsackie, New York State.'

Redfern, New South Wales, Australia, whose post office opened on 1 July 1856, has an equally strong association with the medical theme. A Sydney suburb, it takes its name from William Redfern, born, probably in Canada, about 1774, who spent his early years in Trowbridge, England. In June 1797 after passing the examination of the London Company of Surgeons, he was commissioned as a surgeon's mate on HMS *Standard*. Implicated, with other members of the crew, in the British naval mutiny at the Nore in 1797, Redfern was sentenced to death, reprieved, and in 1801 deported to Australia. He became assistant surgeon in Norfolk Island in 1802 and was pardoned by Governor Philip Gidley King. In 1805 he was an assistant surgeon in a Sydney hospital and later took charge of a hospital at Dawes Point. His professional skill was highly

12 *Medical postmarks*

regarded and he had the reputation of being one of the finest obstetricians in the colony. Farming was another of Redfern's interests and it led to him having a place on the map and his name in the form of a postmark. He retired in 1826 and died in 1833.

The 1967 issue of the US *Directory of Post Offices* records, in Umatilla County, Oregon, the existence of a third-class post office named Helix. Of this word a basic dictionary definition is 'the incurved rim of the external ear'. Why should an American town have a name like that?

If, inspired by its postmark, the collector pursued this inquiry from the realm of anatomy into that of place-name etymology he would uncover a delightful story. Towards the end of the nineteenth century Dr John Griswold, a prominent resident of Umatilla County, attended a patient named Henderson who had developed some kind of ear trouble. The man was sent to nearby Pendleton for treatment. While there, during consultation with another medical man, Dr Griswold used the word 'helix' several times. The novelty of the word appealed to Mr Henderson. He liked the sound of it and remembered it.

Some days later a discussion arose among members of the community as to what name should be given to a new post office which was about to be opened. The name Oxford, originally submitted, had been rejected by the postal administration because of the possibility of confusion with similar names elsewhere. The naming committee had been asked to think again. Mr Henderson had no doubts at all. With an air of infinite wisdom he trotted out his newly acquired item of medical terminology. 'Let's call it Helix,' he suggested. The name at least had the merit of being original. As a place-name it was unlikely to be duplicated. Mr Henderson's proposal was accepted. When the post office was opened on 6 May 1880 with Mary Ann Simpson in the role of postmistress, outgoing letters carried the postmark Helix, primarily because a man in Oregon had trouble with his ear.

Scattered about the world from Nova Scotia to Argentina and in countries as widely separated as New Zealand, Pakistan, Portugal, America and Australia are hundreds of places whose postal imprints have a more than casual connection with the medical profession and the spheres of health and healing. If one wished to begin a collection of postal markings from such places a desirable piece of preliminary planning would be the compilation of a list of typical items one might seek.

Here, compiled from innumerable sources, with brief notes where applicable, is a specimen check list along these lines. It has no pretensions to completeness. Many of the items catalogued would be difficult to obtain; but the schedule contains in basic outline a potential selection of cancellations material which would make any collection of the medical theme one of outstanding interest.

AUSTRALIA

Balmain, New South Wales

Post office opened 1853. Named after William Balmain, (1762–1803) pioneer surgeon and landowner. As assistant surgeon, he arrived at Port Jackson in 1788 and was later transferred to Norfolk Island. In 1796 he was appointed principal surgeon in New South Wales and given a grant of several hundred acres on the western side of Sydney. Part of his original grant is now the suburb of Balmain, Sydney.

Bancroft, Queensland

A town in Burnett district, named after Joseph Bancroft (1836–1894) medical practitioner born at Stretford, Manchester, England. He studied at the Manchester Royal School of Medicine and Surgery, decided to emigrate to Australia and in June 1864 embarked as surgeon on the 523-ton paddle-wheel steamer *Lady Young*. Became visiting surgeon to Brisbane Hospital in 1867 and was for some years health officer for the city. His son, Thomas (1860–1933) also a medical man, of Eidsvold, Queensland, was well known for his work in various branches of natural history and medical investigation.

Bass, Victoria

Seventy miles (112 km) south of Melbourne, near the coast and 15 miles (25 km) from Wonthaggi. Population: about 500. Named for George Bass, eighteenth-century navy surgeon and navigator who discovered Bass Strait in 1798.

Braidwood, New South Wales

Located 188 miles (3000 km) south of Sydney. Post office opened as Strathallen in 1835. Five years later it adopted the middle name of the medical practitioner upon whose land the town was developed.

He was Dr Thomas Braidwood Wilson, born 1792 at Uphall, West Lothian, Scotland. He joined the navy in 1815 and later served as a surgeon-superintendent on convict ships. In 1836 on his eighth voyage to Australia he brought his wife and family to

New South Wales. They settled in the place now called Braidwood where Dr Wilson won respect for farm management and his efficiency as a magistrate.

Brisbane Base Hospital, Queensland

Reputedly one of the largest hospitals in the Southern Hemisphere. The post office occupies part of a white-painted two-storey building which also houses the hospital inquiry office. The building is on 'stilts' with verandahs on both storeys. It looks south over the Victoria Park golf course practice green. The hospital post office is on the corner of Bowen Bridge Road and Herston Road and derives its name from the adjacent hospital.

Canberra, Australian Capital Territory

Special handstamp issued 19 September 1970 for Asian and Australasian Congress of Anaesthesiology.

Collie, Western Australia

Collie, a coal-mining town 125 miles (200 km) south of Perth derives its name from an adventurous Scottish-born naval surgeon, explorer and administrator. He was Alexander Collie, born in 1793 in Aberdeenshire. Collie completed a medical course at Edinburgh and studied surgery in London. Later he accepted an appointment as assistant surgeon in the British navy and sailed for Australia in 1829. His first medical duty at sea was to attend the confinement of Mrs Stirling, wife of Lieutenant Governor Stirling, whose son became an admiral 50 years later. The expedition which put Collie's name on the map was his exploration of the south-western section of Western Australia. It led to the discovery of the rivers Collie and Preston. Collie died in 1835 and a granite monolith stands in his honour in the town that bears his name.

Concord Repatriation General Hospital (now The Repatriation General Hospital), New South Wales

Erected and opened in 1942 as an army hospital. Repatriation department took over from the army in 1947. The post office at this time reverted from a military post office to a civil post office.

In the mid-1960s the hospital had a bed capacity of 1,500 and a staff of 1,800.

Cooper's Plains, Queensland

Post office opened 1 October 1876. Name—a corruption of Cowper's Plains—is derived from Dr Cowper, medical superintendent of the penal settlement established at Moreton Bay, near Brisbane, in 1824.

Douglas Park, New South Wales

Named, in spite of the variation in spelling, in honour of Henry Grattan Douglass MD, MLC (1791–1865) surgeon and magistrate who served in the Peninsular War and in the West Indies. He arrived in Sydney from Britain in 1826. He was assistant surgeon at Parramatta and is noted for his connection with the foundation of Sydney University.

Goulburn Base Hospital, New South Wales

Named after Henry Goulburn (1784–1856) Secretary of State for the Colonies. In 1966 the hospital had 167 beds. It was featured in an appeals postal slogan (1966) with the wording 'Give to the Goulburn Base Hospital Building Appeal'.

Greenslopes Repatriation Hospital, Queensland

From Greenslopes, a Brisbane suburb. Mr F. Wecker who once owned most of the land referred to it as his 'green slopes'. The hospital, then known as 112th Army General Hospital, was constructed during the 1939–45 War as part of a plan to establish Army base hospitals in all the states of Australia. First patients were admitted January 1942. In April 1947 the Repatriation department took over the establishment. In the 1960s the hospital comprised 19 single-storey wards, built on gently sloping terraces.

Heidelberg Repatriation General Hospital, Victoria

Built 1940. Originally 115 Australian General Hospital. Renamed May 1947. Had post office facilities in 1964.

Hollywood Repatriation Hospital, Western Australia

Built 1943 for men and women of Australia's armed forces.

Located amid 25 acres of landscaped gardens about five miles (8 km) from the city, between Perth and the coast. Title changed from 110 (P) Military Hospital to present name in 1947.

Melbourne, Victoria

International Council of Nurses Quadrennial Congress, 1961. Special handstamp.

Melbourne, Victoria

A special circular handstamp was used on 22 February 1971 to mark the occasion of the International Plastic and Reconstructive Surgery Fifth Congress.

Randwick Military Hospital, New South Wales

Post office opened 1917.

Rockhampton Hospital, Queensland

Established 1858. Serves as a base hospital for approximately 90,000 people. Patient accommodation 569 beds.

Royal Melbourne Hospital, Victoria

Established 1842, when it had '. . . four doctors, 20 beds and often no money for bandages'. Now rates as one of the largest and best-equipped teaching hospitals in the Southern Hemisphere. Post office facilities were available here in the 1950s.

Springbank Repatriation General Hospital, South Australia

Suburban area, south of Adelaide. Place-name is descriptive, and dates from 1849. Postmark reads 'R. G. H. Springbank, South Aust'.

Sydney, New South Wales

Over 2,900 articles were postmarked at Sydney University post office over the period 10–16 August 1968 with a special handstamp marking the joint annual meeting of the British Medical Association, the Australian Medical Association and the Third Australian Medical Congress.

Sydney, New South Wales

A 38 mm rubber postmarker was used over the period 22–29 August 1969 at Sydney University in connection with the 11th International Congress of the International Society of Haematology and the International Society of Blood Transfusions.

Ultimo, New South Wales

Post office opened 1 July 1880, closed 1889; re-opened 6 January 1890. A Sydney suburb named for the home of Dr John Harris (1754–1838).

Westwood Sanatorium, Queensland

Established September 1919. An annex to Rockhampton Hospital, with independent post office facilities. Originally a tuberculosis sanatorium. In 1967 it had a bed capacity of 150 with 26 resident staff.

Wooroloo Hospital, Western Australia

Originally built to accommodate tuberculosis cases. Converted to general hospital 1958. The hospital has been likened to a small village. It is sited in the hills away from local suburbia and provides its own community services including facilities for cricket, basketball, football, tennis and swimming. The hospital's post office was listed, 1931, as Wooroloo Sanatorium and as Wooroloo Hospital in 1951. In the 1960s an isolation section was provided for the treatment of white patients suffering from leprosy.

AUSTRIA

International Congress of Occupational Medicine, Vienna

An elaborate special handstamp to mark the 15th Congress was in use from 19–24 September 1966. The first congress on this theme was held in Milan, Italy, in 1906.

CANADA

Doctors Cove, Nova Scotia

The village lies in Shelburne county and its medical name is no accident. In 1764 Simeon Gardner, a native of Nantucket, Massachusetts, arrived in Nova Scotia and settled at Barrington. Gardner had seven children of whom one, Elizabeth, married a Dr Collins of Liverpool, England. Dr Collins set up a practice in the Cape Sable region and his service to the community is still recalled in the name Doctors Cove. Post office closed 4 August 1970.

Essondale, British Columbia

Site of provincial mental hospital. Named after Dr Henry Esson Young, Provincial Secretary when the hospital was established.

Nova Scotia Sanatoruim, Kentville, central Nova Scotia

Government owned and operated tuberculosis sanatorium, completed 1904. Had post office facilities in the 1960s.

Medicine Hat, Alberta

The Indian name was Saamis, meaning the head-dress of the medicine man.

Powell River, British Columbia

Named in honour of Dr Israel Wood Powell (1836–1915) first McGill graduate in medicine to practise on the west coast and first president of the Medical Council of British Columbia. Born in Colborne, Upper Canada, he came to BC in 1862.

Prince Albert Sanatorium, Saskatchewan

Listed as possessing post office facilities in the 1930s. Sanatorium closed c1962; replaced by chest clinic in Victoria Union Hospital. Postmarks prior to closure of the Sanatorium are very rare.

Sanatorium—Bégin, Dorchester county, Province of Quebec

Established 1949, for tuberculosis patients. Named after Monsieur J. D. Bégin, a minister of the provincial parliament who donated the site for the hospital. Resulting from the drop in tuberculosis cases, the sanatorium opened departments for the chronic sick and mentally ill. Has had post office facilities since the 1950s.

EGYPT

Cairo

A special 40 mm circular handstamp was in use in October 1964 to commemorate the first Asian Medical Congress, held in Cairo.

ENGLAND

Benenden Chest Hospital, Cranbrook, Kent

Formerly appeared in postmark form as Benenden Sanatorium. Renamed 1957. Hospital is controlled by the Civil Service (formerly the Post Office) Sanatorium Society.

Blackpool, Lancashire

A double-ring circular handstamp was in use for the Royal Society of Health Congress held in Blackpool, in April 1956, and one in a shield design for the congress held in April 1961.

Blackpool Military Hospital, Lancashire

Listed as having a single-circle handstamp in *A Reference List of British Army Postmarks used in the Great War*, by Rev P.E. Raynor. Appears as town sub-post office in *Post Office Guide*, April 1917.

Bournemouth, Hampshire

Double-ring circular date-stamp in use at Royal Sanitary Institute Congress, April 1955.

British Legion Village, Maidstone, Kent

First appeared in postmark form as Preston Hall, Maidstone, Kent in 1924. In 1925 the British Legion—an organisation founded by Earl Haig for men and women who served in the First World War and subsequent wars—took over Preston Hall. It had started in 1919 as a village settlement for ex-servicemen suffering from pulmonary tuberculosis. The hospital section was taken over in 1948 by the Ministry of Health.

Gosport, Hampshire

In 1689 the first British hospital for naval use was requisitioned at

Plymouth and this practice spread to other ports, including Haslar which was opened in 1754. The nursing was done by women, often the widows of sailors or Royal Marines. The granting of the freedom of Gosport to the Royal Naval Medical Service was commemorated by a special postmark on 11 September 1970. At Haslar Hospital there is a Royal Navy post office with no access for the general public. Opened prior to 1927. Now a town sub-post office of Gosport.

Holloway, Matlock, Derbyshire

Lea Hurst, Holloway was once the home of Florence Nightingale (1820–1910) the English nurse and pioneer of hospital reform. To commemorate this link a special handstamp, incorporating Miss Nightingale's famous lamp, was used at Holloway on 12 May 1970, the 150th anniversary of her birth.

King Edward VII Sanatorium, Midhurst, Sussex

Located about 2½ miles (4 km) north of Midhurst. Sanatorium opened 1906 and incorporated under a Royal Charter in 1913. Patients are received from all over the British Commonwealth and from many other overseas countries. Post office established here about 1908.

Lancaster Moor Hospital, Lancashire

Hospital opened in July 1816 on five acres of land as 'a Lunatic Asylum or House for the reception of Lunatics or other Insane Persons within the County Palatine of Lancaster'. During its first year 60 patients were admitted. The hospital now covers 120 acres and in 1965 its admissions totalled 2,841. It stands 300 feet (91 m) above sea level and its post office, sited in modernised premises which were once the hospital's bakehouse, opened on 1 January 1961.

Lincoln

On October 1970 a special one-day handstamp enclosing the words 'For the Service of Mankind' was in use commemorating the work of the St John Ambulance Association and Brigade. An earlier datestamp linked with this source was the St John Cadet Coronation Camp double-ring special handstamp used at Upminster, Essex, in July and August 1953.

London

Special handstamps were issued by the National Florence Nightingale Memorial Committee and the Florence Nightingale Hospital, London, in May 1970 to commemorate the 150th anniversary of the birth of this pioneer of hospital reform.

London, EC2

A special handstamp was in use 3 June 1970 in connection with the 24th Annual Conference of the Society of Radiographers.

London, SE1

World Congress of Anaesthesiologists. A special postmark to commemorate this international congress was used 9–13 September 1968. The postmark had as its central motif the symbol of the conscious-unconscious.

London, SW

Single-cricle handstamp reading 'Health Exhibition sw' in use 1884.

London, SW

Special double-ring handstamp in use, August 1913, in connection with International Congress of Medicine.

London, SW1

Double-ring handstamp in use for Catholic Doctor's Congress, 9 July 1962.

London, W2

Special handstamp in use 10 September 1967 to commemorate discovery of penicillin in 1928. The design included the names of Sir Alexander Fleming and St Mary's Hospital, Paddington at which he graduated and where much of his research on bacteriology was carried out.

London, WC2

Special handstamp in use 21 July 1972 on letters mailed in special posting box at Royal College of Surgeons, Lincolns Inn Fields, in connection with 25th anniversary of the Faculty of Dental Surgery at the Royal College of Surgeons.

Lostock Hall, Lancashire

In the urban district of Walton-le-Dale, 3 miles (5 km) from Preston; named after a former private residence, converted as a convalescent hospital 15 June 1922. Post office is sited a short distance away, in residential part of the village.

Manor House Hospital, London, NW11

Hospital founded 1917 to provide treatment for war wounded. Its site was the old Manor House of the North End village of Hampstead. Ten years later the land was bought by the Industrial Orthopaedic Society as a step towards the provision of a permanent hospital. On 30 October 1969 a special one-day handstamp was issued to mark the opening by the Duchess of Kent of a new four-storey wing costing over £250,000.

Milford Chest Hospital, Godalming, Surrey

Hospital, originally named Surrey County Sanatorium, was opened in 1928 by Rt Hon Neville Chamberlain. Originally only tuberculous patients were treated. Later the hospital was adopted as a centre for the treatment of all forms of thoracic disease. The post office, run in conjunction with the hospital shop, was started in 1953 to provide a facility for patients and staff.

A League of Friends of Milford Hospital was started in 1955 and administration of the shop and post office was handed over to this body in April 1958, although the hospital secretary retained overall control and held office as sub-postmaster.

Mumps, Lancashire

Former town sub-post office (closed 1971) in Oldham. Name is unconnected with the contagious disease, epidemic parotitis. Its source is believed to be the 'mumpers' or beggars who frequented a nearby workhouse.

Netley Hospital, Southampton
Large military hospital established for care of wounded in the
Crimean War. Post office was in existence here, and handstamps
*c*1901 have been seen.

Orthopaedic Hospital (The), Oswestry, Shropshire
Full title of the hospital is Robert Jones and Agnes Hunt Ortho-
paedic Hospital. Established 1900 in a small Shropshire village.
Now one of the most progressive orthopaedic centres in Europe.
Postmark formerly worded 'Shropshire Orthopaedic Hospital'.

Royal Hospital School, Holbrook, Suffolk
Founded 1694 by William III and Mary as a hospital for old and
disabled seamen. Then became a school for children of seamen,
both boys and girls. Subsequently known as The Greenwich
Royal Hospital. In 1933 the school moved to Holbrook, Suffolk,
where it became known as the Royal Hospital School. Though no
longer classifiable as a medical postmark, the history of this post
office has strong links with the theme.

Royston, Hertfordshire
To mark the centenary of the opening of Royston Hospital the
Royston section of the North Herts Stamp Club sponsored a pic-
torial handstamp and commemorative cover in use on 7 June 1969.

Tonbridge, Kent (Delarue School)
A special postmark was issued on 28 June 1969 to mark the work
carried on at this school founded by the Spastics Society in 1955.
It is the first 'secondary' school in Britain to be devoted entirely
to the education and treatment of cerebrally palsied pupils.

Torquay, Devonshire
Special postmarks have been used to commemorate annual congresses of the Royal Society of Health since 1955. Most of them
have included a replica of the Society's emblem. Torquay was the
venue in 1960 and 1964.

Walton-on-Thames, Surrey

A hospital for the accommodation of New Zealand soldiers wounded on the Western Front established at Walton-on-Thames during the First World War. Distinctive postmarks worded 'New Zealand Sta. Post Office No 4' were in use. Commemorating this link, a modern sub-post office opened 1 December 1958 is in existence in New Zealand Avenue. Military hospitals, with their own wartime datestamps, were also established at Brockenhurst (Hampshire) and Codford (Wiltshire).

West Wellow, Southampton, Hampshire

Issued a special handstamp in May 1970 to celebrate 150th anniversary of the birth of hospital reformer Florence Nightingale.

Wroughton RAF Hospital, Swindon, Wiltshire

Officially, Princess Alexandra's Royal Air Force Hospital, this post office franks certain classes of outgoing mail with a circular date-stamp. On 27 July 1968 a special rectangular handstamp incorporating the Red Cross and an RAF roundel was used to commemorate the 50th anniversary of the Royal Air Force.

GERMANY (Federal Republic of)

Oberkochen, Stuttgart

Special handstamp in use 12 January 1968. (See figure XIV.) The design marked the 100th anniversary of scientific microscope development by Ernst Abbe (1840–1905) and Carl Zeiss (1816–1888).

IRELAND

Hospital, Limerick

A parish and village which owes its origin to the Knights Hospitallers of St John. Irish form of the name: *Ospideal Ghleann Aine*.

NETHERLANDS

Amsterdam

Venue of the 9th International Congress of Internal Medicine, held 7–10 September 1966, for which a special handstamp was in use.

NEW ZEALAND

British Medical Association Conference, Auckland
Special handstamp, 1961.

Cherry Farm, Dunedin
Post office opened 8 September 1969, in canteen of Cherry Farm psychiatric hospital, 3 miles (5 km) south of Waikouaiti on the Dunedin highway. The hospital has provision for about 700 patients.

Cornwall, Auckland
Post office opened 1959 at National Women's Hospital, Cornwall Park.

Dunedin Hospital
Post office opened 1 December 1965, sited in the main hospital building.

Gisborne Health Camp, East Coast
Temporary post office, first opened 1941.

Glenelg Health Camp, Invercargill
Post office opened 1946, of temporary status. Open one day annually at Glenelg Spur.

Hutt Hospital, Wellington
Post office opened 21 February 1972.

Karaka, Auckland
Post office opened 20 December 1965, opposite Kingseat Hospital. The name is derived from that of a tree.

Maheno (Hospital Ship)
One of two hospital ships (see also HS *Marama*) commissioned

during the First World War by the New Zealand government. One
of the ship's medical orderlies was appointed postmaster to handle
mail to and from the ship and a special cancellation was used. At a
stamp auction in New Zealand in May 1967 a registered envelope
date-stamped with the ship's cancellation realised £20.

Marama (Hospital Ship)

The *Marama*, a former passenger liner, was one of two hospital
ships under commission by the New Zealand government between
July 1915 and April 1919 for the conveyance of sick and wounded
soldiers from the battlefields of Gallipoli and France to hospitals
and bases in Egypt, Malta, England and New Zealand. A metal
die cancellation reading 'HS *Marama*, NZ' was in use on the vessel.

Maunu Health Camp, Whangarei

Temporary post office, first opened 1955, five miles west of
Whangarei. Also known as Northland Health Camp.

Middlemore Hospital, Auckland

Post office sited in hospital grounds, opened 13 October 1969. It
serves patients, staff and nearby residents.

Ngawhatu, Nelson

Post office, located 6 miles (10 km) south of Nelson, opened 1932.
Mental hospital.

Otaki Health Camp, Wellington

Temporary post office. First opened 1941.

Pakuranga Health Camp, Auckland

Temporary post office, first opened 1949.

Princess Margaret Hospital, Christchurch

Three miles (5 km) southwest of Christchurch. Post office opened
August 1959. A special commemorative cover was used as a
memento of the event.

Pukeora Sanatorium, Napier

Post office in existence 1920–1932. Three miles (5 km) west of Waipukurau.

Roxburgh Health Camp, Dunedin

Temporary post office, first opened 1941; open one day each year; at Roxburgh.

Roxburgh Hydro, Dunedin

Located 6 miles (10 km) north west of Roxburgh. Post office opened 1949. Closed 6 July 1962.

Silverstream Hospital, Hamilton

Sixteen miles (26 km) from Wellington. Built by Ministry of Works during the Second World War. Post office opened 1944. Hospital taken over by American forces as a base hospital during the Pacific islands campaign. Now administered by Wellington Hospital Board as geriatric unit.

Timaru Hospital

Post office opened 17 March 1969.

Waikato Hospital, Hamilton

Pronounced 'Why katto'. Established as independent hospital district in 1886. First hospital, a small wooden building housing about half a dozen patients, was opened the following year. The post office, located in the hospital buildings, opened 28 September 1959. It serves patients and staff and is under the control of a postmistress employed by the New Zealand Post Office.

Wellington Hospital, Wellington

First Wellington Hospital, at Thorndon, was opened 15 September 1847 on site later occupied by Wellington Girls' College. In the early days there was one doctor and two attendants. A brick and timber two-storey building, it suffered severely in the big earthquakes of 1848 and 1855.

In 1878 work on new hospital on present site began. It was opened in 1881 and contained four wards. In the first year it cared for 100 in-patients, 60 of them Maoris. Included in the hospital's facilities is a modern post office, first opened 16 February 1949.

PORTUGAL

Lisbon

Special handstamp in use 1967 in connection with the 6th European Rheumatology Congress.

Sanatorio de Sousa Martins, Guarda

Located at Guarda, at an altitude of over 3,000 feet, (1,000 m) the sanatorium is one of 13 administered by the *Instituto de Assistencia Nacional Aos Tuberculosos*. The institute was founded in 1899 by the Queen of Portugal. Post office in existence 1965–1968.

SCOTLAND

City Hospital, Edinburgh

Opened as fever hospital 13 May 1903 on a 72-acre (3,000-are) site. The sub-post office, within the hospital grounds, opened in September 1955 and the group secretary and treasurer to the hospital's board of management is the official sub-postmaster.

Glen o'Dee Hospital, Banchory, Kincardineshire

Hospital built in the late nineteenth century and opened in 1900. It was one of the first sanatoria to be opened in Britain. Credit for its foundation is given to Dr David Lawson, one of the first chest physicians in Britain to appreciate the value of x-rays in diagnosis and assessment of tuberculosis of the lungs.

Design of the sanatorium was based on that of similar premises at Nordrach in the Black Forest and for a time the Scottish establishment flourished as Nordrach-on-Dee. Demand for accommodation diminished about 1924 and the sanatorium was closed in 1928. The building lay disused until 1934 when it was converted to a luxury hotel in which capacity it ran until 1941 when it was requisitioned for army billets. In 1945 the Scottish branch of the British Red Cross purchased the building. After reconditioning it was opened in 1949 as a hospital.

A sub-post office was opened under the name Glen o'Dee

Sanatorium on 1 October 1949 and renamed Glen o'Dee Hospital in July 1962. The hospital matron was for many years also the sub-postmistress. The post office finally closed on 31 May 1967.

Kelso, Roxburghshire

On Sunday 29 August 1965, Floors Castle, built by Vanbrugh in 1718 and altered to its present Tudor aspect by Playfair about 1849, was open to the public to raise funds for the National Society for Cancer Relief.

For this occasion, and in successive years for the same cause, a special handstamp depicting the main entrance to the castle was in use. Mail cancelled in this way was posted in an elegant late nineteenth-century pillar box of octagonal design. About 3,500 items were mailed for the 1965 event. A special Diamond Jubilee handstamp was used in 1971. The castle is sited in a spacious setting of woodland and gardens near the junction of the rivers Tweed and Teviot.

Royal Infirmary, Edinburgh, Midlothian

Branch post office, sited within the hospital building, was opened at The Royal Infirmary of Edinburgh on 13 June 1955. The hospital was founded in 1729 largely through the efforts of local physicians and the Lord Provost, George Drummond.

SOUTH AFRICA

Durban, Natal

Double-ring handstamp was in use here 16–21 September 1957 to commemorate the 41st South African Medical Congress.

Elim Hospital, Transvaal

Founded by the Swiss Mission in South Africa in 1896.

Jane Furse Hospital, Transvaal

Named after the little daughter of Bishop Furse, of Pretoria. The child died while her father was in residence. A memorial to her can be seen in Pretoria Cathedral. Post office listed, 1968.

Pietermaritzburg, Natal
Special postmark issued for South African Medical Congress held here, 1936.

Port Elizabeth, Cape Province
A commemorative cancellation was available for the 47th Medical Congress held here in 1954.

Rondebosch, Cape Province
First South African medical congress to be provided with a special date-stamp was held here in 1933.

Salvation, Natal
This post office serves 80 African kraals and the 65-bed Mountain View Bantu hospital. Its mail goes out and comes in by African runner 3 times a week to a point where it is picked up by a motor bus and taken 50 miles (80 km) to the nearest railhead. The hospital caters for Bantu patients over a wide area.

South African Nursing Association, Golden Jubilee Congress, Cape Town
A special commemorative date-stamp, incorporating the badge of the association, was used at the temporary post office during the Congress, held 26–30 October 1964.

SWEDEN

Stockholm
Special handstamp was in use 2 July 1962 to commemorate a Cardio-Vascular surgery congress.

Stockholm
A special handstamp was in use for the 5th World Congress of Fertility and Sterility, June 1966.

UNION OF SOVIET SOCIALIST REPUBLICS
Under the heading 'Sanatorii' 29 post offices are listed in the 1968 edition of the Universal Postal Union's *Nomenclature Internationale des Bureaux de Poste.*

UNITED STATES OF AMERICA

Accident, Garrett County, Maryland

About 1751 a grant of land was given to George Deakins by George II of England. According to the terms Deakins was to receive 600 acres of land anywhere in Western Maryland. He sent two corps of engineers, each without knowledge of the other, to survey the best land. After completing the survey the engineers returned and were surprised to find that they had chosen identical sites. To commemorate this coincidence Deakins named the plot 'The Accident Tract' from which derived the name of the town. The first post office here was established 10 January 1845 with John R. Brooke as the first postmaster.

Barium Springs, Iredell County, North Carolina

Post office, formerly known as Poison Springs, was established 1886. In 1889 the place was developed as a health resort, there being nine springs in the district, and the name was changed to Barium Springs. Now a Presbyterian Home for Children.

Battey State Hospital, Rome, Georgia

Hospital opened 1945. Its name honours Dr Robert Battey (1828–1895) a local physician and surgeon of wide renown. Born in Augusta, Georgia, he moved to Rome in 1836 to work in a drug store owned by his brother. Later he graduated in medicine and surgery and devised a new method of treating babies with club feet. During the Civil War he served as a surgeon with the Confederate forces and later as a hospital surgeon in Atlanta. The hospital that bears his name was built during the Second World War. Its post office, sited inside the hospital buildings, was opened on 20 June 1946 with Mrs Josephine Hoopes as postmistress.

Biggs Hospital, New York

A former rural station post office of Ithaca, New York, closed in the 1950s. The hospital was named for Hermann Michael Biggs (1859–1923) a pioneer of preventive medicine. Biggs was born in Trumannsburg, New York, of English stock, an ancestor, George Biggs having emigrated to America in 1690. He graduated from

Cornell in 1882 and received his MD from Bellevue Hospital Medical College where he became professor of medicine in 1912. In 1894 he introduced the use of diphtheria anti-toxin into USA. The post office which bore his name was one of 121 closed in New York State between 1949 and 1957.

Bromide, Johnston County, Oklahoma

Took its name from nearby mineral springs. Post office established as Juanita. Name changed to Bromide 8 June 1907.

Catawba Sanatorium, Virginia

State tuberculosis sanatorium in Roanoke County. Name Catawba derives from that of an Indian tribe.

Cushing Hospital, Framingham, Massachusetts

Formerly the Cushing Veterans Administration Hospital. Named in honour of Dr Harvey Williams Cushing (1869–1939) noted for his work in neurological surgery.

Doctor Phillips, Florida

A rural sub-post office of Winter Garden, Orange County, opened April 1929. It was named for Dr P. Phillips one of the world's largest growers of oranges, grapefruit and tangerines. Post office closed in the 1960s.

Doctortown, Wayne County, Georgia

According to legend this village was the camp site for one or more Indian tribes, including a number of Indian 'doctors'. From this fact the town derived its name. The post office here closed 20 October 1967. Old maps confirm that the place was known as Doctors Town from a very early date.

Ether, North Carolina

Small community and fourth class post office in northeast section of Montgomery County.

Fisherville, Augusta County, Virginia

Two things make the Woodrow Wilson rural branch postmark of

Fishersville somewhat unusual. First: its source is a rehabilitation centre operated by the Virginia Department of Vocational Rehabilitation. It lies north of Highway 250, 7 miles (11 km) from Waynesboro. Dedicated in November 1947 the centre provides service to the maimed, crippled and afflicted in vocational training, recreation and self-care. About 1,200 students, most of them from Virginia, attend each year. There are about 200 members of staff.

The second point of interest is that in the late 1960s Fishersville's postal marking appeared to perpetuate a spelling error in the place name. Although contemporary official US Post Office lists and other records gave the name as Fishersville, the postmark appeared in the form Fisherville.

Harmon, Lee County, Illinois

Named for Dr Harmon Wasson, prominent physician in a neighbouring town.

Healing Springs, Virginia

Fourth class post office in south central section of Bath County established 3 August 1855. It was named for the thermal mineral spring, the water from which was at one time bottled and sold. Now site of a resort hotel. The old part of the building was used as a hospital during the Civil War.

Homer Folks Hospital, Otsego County, New York

Branch post office of Oneonta. Hospital opened December 1935 as a New York tuberculosis hospital of 200 beds.

Horton, Weston County, Wyoming

Post office, listed in 1937; closed before 1945. The post office was established in the home of Dr Fred Horton, who came to the region in 1890.

Hygiene, Boulder County, Colorado

In 1879 or 1880 Jacob S. Flory settled in this region. He was responsible for building a church and, in 1880, a sanatorium which he called Hygiene Home. He also edited a newspaper *The Home Miner* and in 1883 became the town's first postmaster. The sanatorium for which the village was named was eventually destroyed by fire and in 1950 Hygiene's population had dwindled to 20.

Kodol, Wetzel County, West Virginia
Post office established October 1900; closed between 1965 and 1967. Named after patent medicine called Kodol Dyspepsia Cure.

Lee's Summit, Jackson County, Missouri
On 4 November 1868 the town of Strother was incorporated and renamed Lee's Summit. The name paid tribute to Dr Pleasant Lea, the town's physician. He was shot and killed during the Civil War. Years later when the railroad established a depot here it was named Lee's Summit. Although the doctor's name was mis-spelled the error has remained uncorrected.

Medical College, Richmond, Virginia
Began as medical department of Hampden-Sydney College, 1838. Oldest medical college in state. A station post office of Richmond.

Medical Lake, Washington
Medical Lake's name derives from the mineral properties discovered in the water by American Indians in the late 1840s. The Indians believed the waters to be a cure for rheumatism. The town and lake lie 17 miles (27 km) southwest of Spokane.

During the 1890s and until the early 1920s Medical Lake enjoyed great popularity as a health centre. Its minerals were bottled and distributed far and wide. A State school and a hospital for mental patients are now established in the region.

Medicine Mound, Hardeman County, Texas
Named for four elevations (about 200 ft or 70 m). The mounds were camp and ceremonial sites of the Comanche Indians. Medicinal herbs reputedly grew here in profusion.

Mount Healthy, Hamilton County, Ohio
Branch post office of Cincinnati. The US Post Office Department required a change of name. Mount Healthy was selected to commemorate the inhabitants' escape from a cholera epidemic which scourged the region in 1850.

Naval Hospital, Newport, Rhode Island

Hospital was opened 15 April 1913. In the First World War its facilities were expanded. During the height of the 1918 influenza epidemic more than 1,000 patients were treated. In the Second World War services were extended to a peak of 42 buildings and 1,419 patients in February 1945. Later the hospital became available for treatment of active duty and retired military personnel. Its facilities include a post office, sited in the main hospital building, operated by an employee of the US postal service.

Norfolk Naval Hospital Station, Portsmouth, Virginia

Hospital founded 1827. America's oldest naval hospital. A 17-storey building, it has 800 beds.

Radium, Marshall County, Minnesota

Name chosen to commemorate discovery of radium by Madame Curie.

Salol, Roseau County, Minnesota

Said to have derived its name—that of a chemical compound—from a bottle label, taken at random from a drawer in a druggist's store when the name of the community was under discussion.

San Haven, Rolette County, North Dakota

State tuberculosis sanatorium established here in 1909, on a 2,500-acre game reserve. Named Montair when post office established December 1922 with Dr John G. Lamont, sanatorium superintendent, as postmaster. Renamed San Haven, January 1923.

Sanitarium, Napa County, California

Sanitarium is an unusual but not unique example of an establishment for the treatment of the sick giving its name to a town. There is also, in Tom Green County, Texas, a community with a similar name, but spelt Sanatorium. The story behind California's Sanitarium is that in 1878 a group of Seventh Day Adventists established the Saint Helena Sanitarium in the area and called the place Crystal Springs. The community developed around the institution and in time the name was changed by popular usage to Sanitarium.

State Hospital, Saline County, Arkansas

The Little Rock hospital unit was completed in 1882. A new hospital at Benton was completed in 1931 and a special addition, in modern design, in 1965.

State Hospital, Osawatomie, Kansas

Hospital branch post office sited about 1 mile (1·6 km) northeast of Osawatomie. In appearance the hospital looks like a sixteenth-century English manor house. It is perched on a hill and surrounded by attractive wooded grounds.

Throop, Pennsylvania

Branch post office of Scranton, Lackawanna County. Named as a tribute to Dr Benjamin Henry Throop, pioneer physician when Scranton was a mere hamlet. He lived in a cottage, built in 1847, near Slocum Hollow and became Scranton's postmaster in 1853.

Tripler Army Hospital, Honolulu, Hawaii

Named for Charles Stuart Tripler (1806–1866). US army surgeon, born New York City. He graduated MD at the College of Physicians and Surgeons, New York, in 1827.

Trudeau, Essex County, New York

Named in honour of Dr Edward Livingston Trudeau (1848–1915) pioneer of tuberculosis work in America and founder of the country's first sanatorium for its treatment and of the first laboratory devoted to its study. Trudeau post office closed in the 1950s.

Tuberculosis Hospital, Livingston County, New York

Rural station of Mount Morris; post office closed in 1970.

US Naval Hospital, Philadelphia, Pennsylvania

Hospital was commissioned in June 1935 as a general military hospital for all types of diseases as well as a specialised unit for aural rehabilitation, orthopaedic, neuro-psychiatric and radio-isotope treatment. The post office came into being as a unit of the hospital in 1936 as a contract station operated by naval personnel, usually a chief petty officer or a petty officer, 1st class. In November 1945 this system was discontinued and a classified station, under the US postal service, was installed as a tenant unit of the hospital.

Veterans Administration Hospitals

Established in many American centres with post office facilities and individual postmarks. The collection and study of these forms an interesting sub-section of the Medical Postmarks theme.

Warrenton, Fauquier County, Virginia

Named as a compliment to Joseph Warren, distinguished American general and patriot born 1741. He graduated at Harvard College in 1759, having studied medicine, which he began to practise in Boston at the age of 23, after which he became one of the most eminent physicians in the city. He took an active part in political affairs and possessed a gift for eloquence. He was killed at Bunker Hill, June 1775.

William Beaumont General Hospital, El Paso, Texas

The double-ring postmark carries the abbreviation WBGH. The hospital takes its name from William Beaumont (1785–1853) a United States army surgeon and physiologist who advanced knowledge of digestion by observing the stomach directly through an external opening. His special opportunity to do so occurred in June 1822 when Alexis St Martin, a Canadian trapper, was severely wounded by a shotgun discharged at close range. Beaumont used this opportunity to study digestive processes by means of St Martin's 'open stomach'. The results of his observations were published in 1833.

Willoughby, Lake County, Ohio

At the time of its incorporation in 1834, and at the request of several local doctors, this township was named after Professor Westel Willoughby of the medical school at Fairfield in Herkimer County, New York. The medical school went out of existence in 1874 but Professor Willoughby's name lives on in a thriving town whose population rose from 5,600 in 1955 to 15,000 in 1966.

XVI Special event covers, Newfoundland and USA

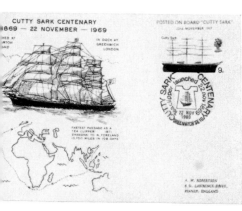

XVII Cutty Sark Centenary and Battle of Britain covers

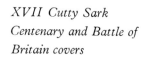

Today, September 3, 1939, Great Britain and France declared war on Germany because Hitler's army attacked Poland. This began the Second World War.

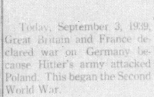

Today, May 8, 1945, at 9.00 A. M., the President of the United States, Harry S. Truman, officially announced that Germany had surrendered unconditionally to the United Nations. Thus the most horrible war in the history of mankind which began on September 1, 1939, came to an inglorious end:

X-ray, Torrance County, New Mexico

Sited 12 miles (19 km) SE of Mountainair. Post office 1917–1920.

Wood Memorial Hospital, Arcadia, De Soto County, Florida

Two Royal Air Force pilots who were killed during training in America gave their names to the two main divisions of the Wood Memorial Hospital, a 1,800 bed state mental hospital in Florida. The pilots' surnames were Carlstrom and Dorr. Every year a special service is held in the town of Arcadia, 7 miles (11 km) from the hospital, in memory of the two men and other RAF pilots who trained at nearby air force bases. The hospital itself was established in 1946.

WALES

Adelina Patti Hospital, Swansea

Named after the eminent Anglo-Italian opera and concert singer (1843–1919). A former town sub-post office of Swansea; post office now closed.

Cardiff, Glamorganshire

Special bi-lingual handstamp in English and Welsh in use 19 November 1971 to commemorate official opening of the Welsh National School of Medicine, University Hospital of Wales.

King Edward VII Sanatorium, Brecon

The post office here was built by patients trained in carpentry by the Sanatorium's own instructor. It was opened in 1930 and for well over 30 years the man in charge was a former patient. The Sanatorium itself was opened by King George V in July 1920 on the Pontywal site acquired in 1913. The property included a mansion and 373 acres of land, the house later being used as a training centre for carpentry. Later it was altered to accommodate male nursing and domestic staff.

Pen-y-val Hospital, Abergavenny, Monmouthshire

A sub-post office of Abergavenny, opened 30 September 1951 and run in conjunction with the hospital shop and café. The hospital itself was established in 1852 and is associated with Maindiff Court Hospital where the former Nazi leader Rudolf Hess was detained for a considerable period during the Second World War.

YUGOSLAVIA

Osijek, Croatia
Medical congress special triangular postmark, May 1965.

Zagreb, Croatia
World Health Day and Medical Congress special handstamp, April 1961.

At one time or another it is probable that every one of the places appearing in the foregoing list possessed its own postmark. Many still do. Even the rare items are probably obtainable by diligent search and inquiry. Moreover, new outlets within this category are constantly appearing.

To gather a really comprehensive collection along these lines, taking a check-list such as this as a basic guide, would be a most fruitful and fascinating exercise. It would reveal on a world-wide scale many absorbing background stories. Written up and illustrated by examples of many of the postal cancellations these would present a unique picture of the link between medicine and the world's postal services.

Perhaps this helps to explain why doctors and surgeons as a professional group are numbered among the most dedicated and enthusiastic collectors of postmarks and postal history material.

14
Postmark Values

The effects of inflation in the western world tend to vitiate attempts to arrive at a realistic assessment of present-day postmark values. In Britain, for example, prices approximately doubled during the period 1950–1970. For this reason it is probably better, in this chapter, to rove over the scene as it was in the recent past and glance at a few specimen valuations at various periods of time rather than attempt to predict what prices are likely to prevail when these words are read at some unknown future date.

During the period immediately before the Second World War, Britain's Postmark Club used as a basis among its members a unit called a 'mark' and it was for many years possible to buy interesting and sometimes quite rare material at prices ranging from one 'mark' to, say, 36 'marks' (2½p in decimal currency).

By the middle 1930s interest in postal markings and notably in pre-stamp letters had reached a stage where it was worthwhile to hold public auctions of material other than adhesive postage stamps. Reporting one such auction (but not, as stated, the *first*) the London newspaper *The Sunday Times* of 11 October 1936 stated:

Thirty philatelists, three of them women, spent yesterday afternoon in a London sale room bidding at the first auction ever held of rare postal marks.

Postmarks date back to the middle of the seventeenth century and were the receipt stamps for postage dues before the coming of the adhesive stamp.

Because nobody knows their value these early bidders at the first auction sale were able to secure marks for a few shillings which later may realise hundreds of pounds.

Many of the marks were on complete letters dating from 1662 and bearing the mark of Henry Bishop, to whom the postal services were then farmed out, and who devised a dating stamp because the public complained that their letters were not being delivered.

As yet comparatively few collectors have troubled with the study of postal history but their number is growing.

Bundles of covers were sold at prices which worked out at about one shilling (5p) each, but £6 15s (£6·75) was paid for the original Exchequer warrant which was the receipt for payments for carrying Royal letters, and signed by William Burghley, first Lord Cecil, famous Elizabethan politician.

There was also a number of interesting ship letters carried by old sailing packets and addressed to various merchants at The Flying Horse, Cornhill and The Jamaica Coffee House in Fleet Street where early eighteenth-century traders gathered to transact business.

The prize among campaign letters was one from the Peninsular War dated 15 September 1811. It was from the Duke of Wellington, signed, to Admiral Berkeley and included the phrase, 'We ought under the existing circumstances to have a large fleet . . .'

The postmark 'Belvedire Place', for some time a mystery to experts, was later identified as the King's Bench Division's own post office and used for the letters of judges.

There were also in the sale letters from young officers describing their baptism of fire in the Napoleonic and other campaigns and some, bearing the 'certificate of purification', which had been pierced by a dagger to release pestilential air which might have carried plague or disease.

When the auction ended for the day about £500 had changed hands.

This newspaper report, apart from its general interest value, places on record remarkable proof of the enhanced values of postal items that were to take place within the next decade. At a postal history auction held in 1945 the identical exchequer warrant referred to as having changed hands at £6 15s (£6·75) came under the hammer again. This time its purchaser paid £17.

In spite of the incredibly low prices obtaining at this time it nevertheless marked the beginning of a definite commercial interest in postmark values in Britain.

On Monday 8 June 1936 at a sale room near Oxford Circus, London, the collection of one of Britain's foremost postmark enthusiasts, Mr James Herbert Daniels, of Brighton, came up for sale. For many years Mr Daniels had carried out pioneer research in this field of philatelic study. As the author of an illustrated history of British postmarks he had become widely-known as an authority on his subject and as a guide and kindly counsellor to collectors of British postmarks he was held in high regard.

His collection, representing a life-long labour on a subject close to his heart, contained hundreds of thousands of items, including a fine series of Bishopmarks from 1663 onwards (see figure I), a contemporary official proclamation of the appointment of Henry Bishop, of Henfield, Sussex, on 16 January 1660 to the post of His Majesty's Postmaster-General, and a House of Lords 1d envelope of April 1840.

Also on offer were a splendid example of the Essex 'slogan' postmark of 1674 and such items as beam type letter scales, Victorian stamp boxes, early china and pottery inkwells and quill pens, fob seals, wafers, early envelopes and notepaper and various framed prints and engravings, all of postal interest.

A letter from St Osyth, Essex, dated 19 January 1674 and bearing a very fine impression of the postmark ESSEX POST GOES AND COMS EVERY DAY—then, as now, of great rarity—was sold for £11 10s (£11·50). The historic proclamation of Bishop's appointment as Postmaster-General realised £6. A selection of over 200 Bishopmarks on entires, dating from 1663, fetched £23. A collection of 330 town marks on entires, dating from 1704 to 1799, realised £16 and an assortment of sailors' and soldiers' letters of the Napoleonic and Crimean War periods, including various sundries in one large album, was knocked down to a fortunate bidder for a total of £75. Various Irish postmarks in two albums, including material relating to the Easter 1916 Dublin uprising, went for £16. The total collection, at a time when public interest in postal markings was just beginning to make itself apparent, realised a little over £1,100.

13 Selection of special event handstamps, Great Britain

14 Special event covers, Great Britain

But this was merely a beginning. In 1945 a London firm of philatelic and postal history auctioneers offered for sale the noteable collection amassed by Mr C. F. Dendy Marshall (1872–1945). The collection virtually amounted to a complete history of the British Post Office. It included practically everything connected with the carriage of mails that could conveniently be housed in an individual collection.

The sale realised nearly £10,000. For one item, a wreck cover of 1875 sent from London to the United States, a price of £17 was reached—a good price in the context of contemporary values. For a single envelope of 1876, despatched from the United States Consulate at Callao, Peru, to an address in Georgia the sum of £30 was paid. A collection of English and 'used abroad' cancellations and adhesives found a purchaser at £235.

In February that same year material from the collection of Samuel Graveson, of Hertford, England, came under the auctioneer's hammer, on the occasion of the collector's 76th birthday. For 40 years of his busy life Mr Graveson had been connected with the printing and publishing industries. His interest in postal history began in 1931 and he became a founder member of the (British) Postal History Society. In 14 years he had gathered what was reportedly one of the finest collections of postal research material ever assembled.

It included (valuation £15) a letter, *c*1327, from Thomas, Cardinal of Naples, to the Archbishop of Salzburg—a fine example of a letter of the period when the Roman Church had its own letter carriers—and a fifteenth-century letter (valuation £10) inscribed with the symbol of a crook, cross and chalice, probably indicating that it was conveyed by one of the Knights of St John of Jerusalem.

Another item, valued at £50 in the catalogue, consisted of an original letter dated 1419, during the reign of King Henry v, from the Ambassadors of England appointed for the treaty between England and Flanders made after the battle of Agincourt. An important historical document, decorated with the Seals of the Ambassadors, it addressed '*Les Honnourables et Saiges Echevins et Conseil de la Ville de Gand*' on the subject of the continuation of the truce between the two countries.

An original copy of the issue of *Mercurius Publicus* for 19–26 September 1661 containing an 'advertisement from His Majestie's Post-office' notifying the introduction of the first handstruck stamp, which was to become commonly known as the Bishopmark, was modestly valued at £5 and a selection of 6 packet letters from Paris to London, conveyed by sailing ships in 1727 was priced at a mere £2.

Since that date values have risen in a spectacular way.

Thus, a single envelope of 1872 from the collection of the late E. Egley, of West Park, Leeds, realised £775 at an auction in London in 1952 because of its rare and exotic postal markings, and in 1968 £440 was bid for a 1709 pre-adhesive entire letter from Estonia bearing a rare handstruck marking. About the same time prices of £280 and £360 were realised for certain rare Norwegian cancellations and in November 1968 an eighteenth-century Dublin Dockwra pre-adhesive cover fetched £500.

In December 1964 a vertical strip of five two-soldi Tuscany stamps on a cover of the 1850s with a rare spider's web cancellation in red realised £10,500 and three years later a Swedish item comprising a cover despatched in 1856 from Sweden to the captain of a brig in Buenos Aires was sold for £3,500. The item bore five postage stamps and fetched about £1,500 more than the face value of the individual stamps. At this time the valuations placed on early manuscript postal markings on items relating to the seventeenth- and eighteenth-century colonial posts of North America varied between £50 and £150 per item, with early handstamps from the same region ranging in price from £15 to £350.

Four years later, 47 letters despatched from Paris, France, by balloon post in 1870 by a young Scots surgeon to his sweetheart in York, England, during the siege of Paris in the Franco-Prussian War realised between £6 and £27 each at a New Bond Street auction.

Evidence that interest and prices are being well-maintained has continued into the 1970s. Even relatively commonplace items have tended to appreciate in value. A Glasgow Exhibition special handstamp of 1901, of the type provisionally valued at £2 10s

Matchbox postmarks

(£2·50) when G. R. Pearson published his useful *Special Event Postmarks* in 1963, was sold for £8 in 1972. A Royal Show, Cambridge, England, special handstamp of 1894 valued at £4 in 1963 was listed at £12 after a similar passage of time.

In the early summer of 1972 an envelope addressed by a Yorkshire Member of Parliament to his son in Leeds in 1840 was sold for £900 in a Bournemouth sale room. The envelope was one of a batch of 1,840 covers addressed by Edward Baines, MP (1774–1846) to his son. This particular cover happened to bear the date 6 May 1840—the first day of issue of the famous Penny Black. The authenticating postmark undoubtedly led to this high valuation. Another cover, postmarked 18 January 1840, sold for £650 and two others dated 20 January and 20 February 1840 fetched £450 each. In all, 5 covers realised a total of £3,075.

The envelopes had remained in the family for more than 130 years without anyone realising their value.

15
Societies and Clubs

Most people are gregarious by nature and part of the pleasure of any collecting hobby is the sharing of one's finds and experiences with fellow enthusiasts. In the sphere of postmark collecting membership of a society or club is one of the most satisfactory ways of fulfilling this purpose.

Practically every philatelic society—and they are worldwide and numerous—has its devotees of the postmark as a subject of special study. But in addition there are many societies which exist largely or exclusively for the postal historian and the cancellations specialist.

The growth and development of these organisations may, indeed, be a revealing indication of the rapid and widespread extension of interest in a subject which, in Britain and America in the nineteenth century, claimed the attention of only a handful of active collectors.

The range of societies available is extraordinarily diverse. It includes small groups whose particular study is limited to the postal markings and postal history of a narrow geographical locality no larger than a village, town or county; it also covers more ambitious societies whose area of interest may be the cancellations of an entire state or continent.

A special aspect of postmark collecting is that individual collectors can contribute so much to the general pool of available knowledge. It is like belonging to an amateur dramatic society in which everyone has a part to play. The role may be a small one, a walking-on part; or it could be a star role, demanding much from the player.

People with quite modest abilities in scholarship and research are capable of making really worthwhile discoveries in the sphere of postal history because the field is so wide and so much that is worthy of inquiry and exploration is still unrevealed and unrecorded.

Moreover, the urge to pursue matters by on-the-spot investigation is easily fulfilled and can add so much to the collector's background knowledge. In this way the beginner might set out by acquiring—as the present writer did—an old picture postcard and end by adding to his collection a humble 'find' of considerable human interest.

Here is an extract from a brief personalised account of a visit to a place in Yorkshire, England, known locally by the name Crockey Hill:

If you drive through Crockey Hill, York, one day and find it marked by a bright new road sign, the postmark on an old picture postcard will have helped to put it there. It all began when I added to my postmark collection the impression of a rubber handstamp which read CROCKEY HILL YORK 28 NOV 18.

The postmark was impressed across a KG V penny postage stamp on a birthday greeting card addressed to Miss Gwen Marshall, The Poplars, Scropton Road, near Tutbury, Burton-on-Trent. The card was from Gwen's Aunt Pollie who lived at Deighton, Yorkshire, and it turned up in 1968 on a junk stall in London from whence, in the course of time, it found its way into my collection.

That could have been the end of the matter. But it was not. I decided to look into Crockey Hill's postal history and see what I could find out by an on-the-spot inquiry. I looked the place up in various reference books. Few of them had anything to say about Crockey Hill. *Bartholomew's Gazetteer* said it was 3 miles (5 km) from Escrick (which it is) and that it has a post office (which it has not).

I decided to investigate further, and set out in my car from Scarborough on the breezy East Coast on a blazing hot day in July. An acquaintance at Fulford, York, from whom I made inquiries told me I might have difficulty in finding Crockey Hill. The hamlet was just a mile or two further along the road, 'But,' he told me, 'it's not much more than a dot on the map. It's got no village sign and if you're not careful you'll be through Crockey Hill and on your way somewhere else before you know you've arrived.' I told him I wanted to find out where the post office had been sited and who ran it, when it existed. 'In that case,' said my Fulford friend, 'you want Charlie Lewis at the forge. That's where the post office used to be.' I found the forge. And I found Charlie Lewis.

The forge was an agricultural engineering workshop with a difference. The difference being that it was meticulously planned, attractive to look at and spotlessly clean. The kind of place where you'd hesitate before dropping a spent matchstick.

Charlie Lewis was different, too. He was the sprightliest, brightest most cheerful blacksmith I've ever met. He and his son, John, went out of their way to be helpful.

They told me that there had, indeed, been a post office at Crockey Hill several years ago. Charlie's mother, Mrs Edith Lewis who was 89 on 21 June 1969 and his late father, William, who died in 1954, had been in charge of it.

'They took over the post office here in 1911,' Charlie told me, 'and they ran it until it closed in July 1954. As well as being a craftsman blacksmith, my father was the local postman. He did a daily "walk" of about 12 miles. He was one of a family of 10 of whom seven are still living, the youngest of them being 78.' Then, turning to his son, John, he said: 'See if you can find that old post office sign.'

After a bit of a search the sign, bright and clean as the day it last adorned the old smithy post office, was produced for my inspection. 'My father had it specially made at Wolverhampton,' said Charlie. 'What are you going to do with it?' I asked.

It seemed a pity, having resurrected the sign, to cast it back into the smithy's dark recesses, to be lost and forever forgotten. Charlie considered the matter for a moment. 'I'll tell you what we might do,' he said. 'We could cut off the words "post office" and leave the name Crockey Hill on the sign. Then I could set it up on a piece of my land by the roadside so that folks would know they've arrived at Crockey Hill.'

I left Charlie Lewis and his son contemplating the possibility of putting Crockey Hill right back where it belonged—on the map.

16 The lure of distant places

This is the kind of experience that can add a great deal to a private collector's enjoyment of the postmark-research hobby. In a modest way it can contribute to the philatelic and local history knowledge of others if one's findings are shared with fellow collectors through membership of a club or society.

By joining a study group of this type one can help to disseminate discoveries and perhaps be encouraged to publish one's findings for the benefit of a wider public. There are many other advantages including opportunities for the exchange of material, the pleasure of sharing one's interest and the chance to hear the viewpoints of fellow members and visiting speakers.

An introductory leaflet published in September 1931 tells the basic background story of one such society, the (British) Postmark Club, and provides interesting comment on the values and prices prevailing at that time. It runs:

The Postmark Club, founded about 1883, is a private association for promoting the study and collection of postmarks. It is under the control of a secretary who conducts its entire business.

It is his duty to receive contributions of specimens from members and to arrange for their circulation: to keep and render accounts of sales and purchases, to receive money from buyers and to remit it to sellers; to circulate information that he may consider of interest to collectors.

The subscription is two shillings yearly, payable in advance on 1 October. This money is the property of the Secretary, who in return provides the necessary stationery, etc., and pays postage on each packet when first sent out, on accounts when first rendered and on receipts. Members must pay any further postage incurred on their behalf.

A packet is sent out about the middle of each month from October to June; the Secretary has first choice and arranges the order in which other members see the packet so as to give, as far as possible, equality of position to all in turn; he may change the order of circulation if and when it appears to be to the advantage of members generally to do so.

Packets must be sent on within two days of being received and a member causing excessive and avoidable delay may forfeit his right to see the next packet, or his priority of position if the Secretary shall so decide.

The Secretary may withhold from the packet any contribution too large or heavy for convenient inclusion, or containing specimens unsuitable or grossly over-priced; members must price their own specimens using a unit called a 'mark' worth one sixth of a penny (pre-decimal currency); thus, three marks equals ½d, 12 marks equals 2d, and so on. Specimens may be sent loose but usually sell better if mounted; if loose they must be put into strong envelopes or wrappers; in all cases the nature and value of the contents must be stated on the outside, with the name of the owner and the date of the packet for which they are intended. The Secretary accepts no liability for loss or damage to specimens while in his charge or in circulation. Members taking specimens must initial spaces in the case of mounted specimens and must enter the number taken and the value in marks on each containing wrapper; they must also enter the value in marks on the sheet provided for this purpose with each packet.

Accounts are rendered quarterly and must be paid within seven days: delay in payment involves the Secretary in much needless labour and inconvenience and he reserves the right to exclude any defaulting member from the privileges of the Club.
G. Brumell, Secretary.
September 1931.

It is relevant to note that Mr Brumell, a well-known collector and authority on British postmarks, who died in May 1950, was himself the author of several specialist articles and books on the subject including the widely quoted *Postmarks of the British Isles,* published in 1930, and *British Post Office Numbers 1844–1906,* published in 1946.

The Postmark Club, whose rules and services have of course been updated many times since 1931, is still in existence and flourishing. In common with other similar societies its membership has, in fact, had to be restricted in order to keep its secretarial responsibilities and general management within reasonable bounds. It may, indeed, be symptomatic of the spread of interest in the subject that many societies are obliged to restrict their membership in this way.

In the following list brief details are given of some of the hundreds of clubs and societies which exist to promote the study and collection of postal markings and postal history material.

Alba Stamp Group

Founded 1970. A member of the Association of Scottish Philatelic Societies. Monthly publication: *Scottish Stamp News*. Honorary Secretary: Stanley K. Hunter, 34 Gray Street, Glasgow G3 7TY, Scotland.

American Society of Polar Philatelists, The

Has about 500 members (1970) from 27 countries who collect, exchange and study Arctic and Antarctic postal history material. Publishes *Ice Cap News* which features illustrations of covers, cachets and postal markings. Secretary (1970) Joseph L. Lynch, jr, 213 Clay Drive, Pittsburgh, Pennsylvania, 15235, USA.

Australian Commonwealth Collectors Club

Treasurer: T. W. Ilbery, 8 Bellevue Avenue, Greenwich, New South Wales 2065, Australia. Publish a monthly bulletin which gives coverage to postal history and postal markings of Australia.

Bahamas Postal History Study Circle

There are several groups of serious students who make a study of Bahamas postal history. These groups are composed of men and women throughout the world whose special interest lies in collecting Bahamas mail, past and present. The circle is affiliated with the British Caribbean Philatelic Study Group.

British Postmark Society, The

Formed 1 January 1958. Membership, originally 17, expanded quickly and reached 50 within 4 months of the founding of the Society. In 1970 it totalled 356 members. The aim of the Society is to promote the study of modern British postmarks. A quarterly bulletin is issued and facilities for the exchange of postmark material are provided. Honorary Secretary: T. M. Richards, Portman Hotel, Ashley Road, Boscombe, Bournemouth, BH1 4LT, England.

British West Indies Study Circle

Founded 1954. Membership (home and overseas): about 300. Secretary: P. T. Saunders, Little Caymans, Kingsthorne, Hereford, England. Publishes a quarterly bulletin.

Canada Co-op PMCC

Canadian postmark collector's club originally formed 1945 by the publishers of *The Western Producer*, a Saskatchewan farm weekly newspaper. Open to all postmark collectors on an exchange basis, operated for 25 years. In November 1970 re-organised as the Canada Co-op PMCC. Formation of off-shoot organisation, 'Prairie Postmarkers', for Western Canadians was under consideration in 1972.

Channel Islands Specialists' Society, The

Membership: about 350. Founded 1950 as Channel Islands Study Circle, with about 12 members. Present name adopted, 1951. Publish bi-monthly bulletin and works on Channel Islands stamps and postal history. Exchange packet circulated. Secretary: William Newport, Farm Cottage, 33 Halfway Street, Sidcup, Kent, England.

Covers and Postal Stationery Exchange Club

Runs an exchange packet in two sections: Great Britain, and Commonwealth/Foreign.

East Anglia Postal History Study Circle

(Including Essex Postal History Society).
Honorary Secretary: G. Stephenson, 47 King Street, Royston, Hertfordshire, England.

Federation of Postal History Societies, The

Founded jointly by the Postal History Society and the Society of Postal Historians. The Federation was established January 1968. Main purpose is to circulate information on GB postal history to all members. A bulletin, *The Postal History News*, is circulated quarterly. Secretary: W. R. Wellsted, 23 Shelley Close, Langley, Buckinghamshire, England.

Forces Postal History Society, The

Founded 1952. Membership: over 200. Publish a newsletter. Honorary Secretary: W. Garrard, 7 Hill Beck Way, Greenford, Middlesex, England.

Guild of Saint Gabriel (Great Britain and Ireland)

Membership 245. A society for collectors of postal material on religious subjects. Publishes a bulletin, *Gabriel*. Secretary: J. Eusebio, 66 Greenways, Esher, Surrey, England.

Hovermail Collectors' Club

Honorary secretary: C. J. Richards, 30 Milverton Road Winchester, Hants., England.

London Postal History Group

Founded 27 February 1971. Objective: the promotion of the study of London postal history. Publication: *London Postal History Note-book*. Membership: 45. Secretary: M. M. English, 50 Somerden Road, Orpington, Kent, BR5 4HT, England.

Malta Study Circle, The

Originally formed by a small group of enthusiasts in 1948. Re-formed December 1955. Members later totalled about 250. Publishes a bulletin, *Malta Newsletter*. Study papers are composed and postal auctions held. Secretary: G. Dougall, 29 Stockwell Park Road, London sw9, England.

Maritime Postmark Society

American non-profit-making international collectors' organisation with members in more than 25 different countries.Founded 1939. Formerly known as the International Seapost Cover Club. Its aim is to cater for beginners, average and advanced collectors. The accent is on ship postmarks and related postal markings especially paquebot handstamps. Issues bi-monthly journal, *The Seaposter*. Secretary (1970): Alan T. Tattersall, 7524 103rd Street, Jacksonville, Florida, USA.

Meter Stamp Study Group

Secretary: J. C. Mann, 19 Chartham Road, London SE25 4HN,

SOME OF THE DISTINCTIVE TYPES OF MALTESE CROSSES

SCOTLAND CHANNEL ISLES LEEDS MANCHESTER MULLINGAR WOTTON UNDER ED

NORWICH & PLYMOUTH YORK KILMARNOCK DUBLIN BELFAST CORK

The information on this card compiled by The Great Britain Philatelic Society

17 Types of Maltese Cross cancellations

England. Members collect, exchange and discuss franking mar and machines from all over the world.

Names Society, The

General Secretary: Leslie Dunkling, 7 Aragon Avenue, Tham Ditton, Surrey, KT7 OPY, England. Members are interested names, including postal place-names. Membership 350 in countries. Publishes *Viz*, a bi-monthly journal.

New Zealand Society of Great Britain

Devoted to study of the postage stamps and postal history of N Zealand and its dependencies. Founded 1952; 150 members 1965. Official journal, *Kiwi*, six times a year. Secretary: Cyril Gilders, 10 Southspring, Avery Hill, Sidcup, Kent, Englan

Pacific Islands Study Circle of Great Britain, The

Publishes a circle magazine, *Pacifica*. Secretary: A. E. You 58 Livesay Crescent, Worthing, Sussex, England.

Philometer Society, The

American society devoted to the interests of collectors of machi meter marks. Publishes a monthly bulletin, *The Philometer*

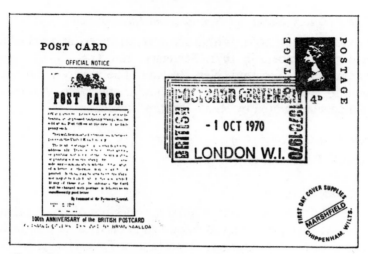

18 100th anniversary of the British postcard

Pioneer Postmarkers' Group

A Canadian group interested in corresponding and exchanging postmarks. Preliminary meeting held at Viscount, Saskatchewan, Canada, 21 May 1972.

Polar Postal History Society of Great Britain

Secretary (1972): H. E. J. Evans, Court House, Court Lane, Cosham, Portsmouth, Hants, England. Publication: *Polar Post*.

Postal Cancellations Society, The

American collectors' society founded 1935. Merged with the Postmark Collectors' Club, February 1950.

Postal History Society, The

Premier British society for the study of postal history, with world wide membership of about 400. Inaugurated 1936 with object of co-ordinating the researches of postal history students. Publishes a bi-monthly bulletin and authoritative handbooks on many aspects of postal history. Secretary: W. R. Wellsted, 23 Shelley Close, Langley, Buckinghamshire, England.

Postal History Society of New Zealand Incorporated

Founded August 1964. Within six weeks membership reached 80. Had 334 members in 1971. Secretary: Rev J. S. G. Cameron, PO Box 1605, Auckland, New Zealand. The society publishes a monthly journal, *The Mail Coach* and monographs written by members and edited by R. M. Startup, FRPSNZ.

Postal History Society of the Americas

Publish *The Postal History Journal*.

Postmark Club, The

Founded about 1883 with original membership of 20. A private association for promoting the study and collection of postmarks. Packets containing members' contributions for exchange are circulated by post. Membership limited to 36. Honorary Secretary: R. Ward, 48 Banner Cross Road, Ecclesall, Sheffield, S11 9HR, England.

Postmark Collectors' Club, The

Founded 1941 by Charles E. Strobel; reorganised 1946 by the Rev Walter A. Smith. An international organisation of collectors of postmarks, all types of postal cancellations, postal markings and allied items. Issues a monthly bulletin, first published October 1946. Membership: 978 in 1972. Director and publisher of bulletin: Herbert H. Harrington, PO Box 87, Warren, Ohio, 44482, USA. Holds an annual convention and has a mobile postmarks and postal history museum in Seneca County, Ohio, USA.

Railway Philatelic Group

Membership: 350. Publishes a society journal. Secretary: R. A. Kirk, 59a Hartley Road, Kirkby-in-Ashfield, Nottingham, NG17 8DS, England.

Registration Label Society

United Kingdom. Founded in the 1960s. Revived in 1967. Secretary: Rev W. G. West, 12 Manor Park Road, Nuneaton, Warwickshire, England.

Societies and Clubs

Rhodesian Study Circle

Founded 1948. Membership: 40. Secretary: F. C. Donaldson, 14 Makepeace Avenue, Highgate, London N6 6EJ, England.

Scottish Postmark Group, The

Founded 1952. Headquarters: Edinburgh, Scotland. Publications: (Handbooks) include: *The Dotted Circle Cancellations of Scotland, Experimental Duplex Cancellations of Scotland, St Kilda—Its Posts and Communications, Scots Local Name Stamps, Mileage Marks of Scotland, Post Offices in Scotland.* Object: The study and clarification of the postal markings of Scotland. A sub-section of the Scottish Philatelic Society.

Society of Postal Historians

Great Britain. Restricted membership of 150 fellows, members and associates. Publication: *Postscript.* Secretary (1972): E. G. Lovejoy.

South African Postmark Society, The

Founded May 1969. President (1972): Dr T. B. Berry. Secretary: Dr H. R. Horne, PO Box 4584, Johannesburg, South Africa. Publishes a bi-monthly newsletter well illustrated with examples of handstamps and machine cancellations. Membership of society open to all who are interested in South African postal markings and postal history.

Thailand Postal History Study Group

Founded 1957. Secretary: P. E. Collins, 88 St John's Road, Woking, Surrey, England.

TPO and Seapost Society

Founded 1938. Restricted membership. Secretary: Cyril Kidd, 9 Beech Park Avenue, Northenden, Manchester, England.

Welsh Philatelic Society

Formed February 1971 to cater for collectors of all types of Welsh postal history and philatelic material. A quarterly bulletin is issued.

Honorary Secretary: A. H. Morgan, B54, Neuadd, Cwrt Maw Waunfawr, Aberystwyth, Cardiganshire, Wales, SY23 3AN.

Yorkshire Postal History Society, The

Founded November 1957. Affiliated to the Philatelic Congress Great Britain and the Yorkshire Philatelic Association. Publish a bulletin *Yorkshire's Post*, first issued in June 1958. Secreta (1971): W. A. Sedgewick, 25 Hunters Lane, Sheffield, S13 8 England.

The foregoing list is far from complete and is intended only a general guide to the type of organisations which have been, are now, available to postmark collectors and postal historians various parts of the world.

New societies and study groups are constantly being formed ai details of these usually appear in the columns of the philate press.

To check the current existence of a particular society cateri for one's special interests, reference to the editor of a philate magazine or, in Great Britain, to the Secretary of The Briti Philatelic Association (446 Strand, London WC2 ORA) is recoi mended. A directory of philatelic societies is published by t British Philatelic Association.

16
Looking Ahead

This book began on a personal note and on a personal note I propose to end. This is because, when everything relevant has been said about a pastime-study subject it [is still, perhaps, the prerogative of the individual collector to attempt to express what it is about the topic that particularly appeals to him.

To my way of thinking postmarks and the matters surrounding them are a magic bridge linking people, places and social customs throughout the world. They are symptomatic of a miraculous chain of world communication, a link between past and present, a memento of the passing scene, an aperitif to one's dormant sense of surprise.

They are a means of enabling one to become better informed on such varied subjects as geography, postal history, place-name origins, social conditions, medicine and surgery, biography, military and naval matters, exploration, art, science and sociology and a multitude of other topics.

Through studying them, one may become better acquainted with local lore and the way people live in faraway places. They encourage inquiry and personal exploration and stimulate interest in things one might otherwise tend to take for granted.

One has, nevertheless, a sense of inadequacy about attempting within the limits of a single volume to cover so vast a subject. When all the things one meant to say have been set down and compressed within the pages of a book one is conscious that a hundred thousand things remain unsaid.

One has left untold the story behind the anniversary postmark of Flatholm Island—where in 1897 Marconi and Kemp conducted experiments in 'telegraphy without wires', transmitting for the first time test wireless signals across water between two countries—and the stories of thousands of postmarks with tales of equal lustre to tell.

One has left unexpressed the bond of companionship that can arise between collectors in far distant places: the friendly appreciative glow that the arrival of a fat, bulging packet of covers from Florida, New Zealand, British Columbia or Singapore can evoke.

One has left unwritten a thousand fascinating factual items which many years of attachment to the topic have encouraged one to accumulate in overflowing files.

It is aggravating to feel that so much has been left unsaid, yet in attempting to give a disciplined presentation of a subject, much that it might be attractive to include must of necessity be omitted.

My personal feeling, looking ahead, is that there will some day be splendid scope for the compilation of a world-embracing encyclopaedia of unusual postal markings. Much pioneer work has been done in this field: all that is required is a co-ordinated effort to draw the threads together. There is more than sufficient material about to provide a firm basis for such a work.

It is a story in which we may see old and accepted ideas discarded and new, unproven ones take their place. Such a change was introduced on 25 January 1912 with the installation of a 'newfangled machine' which came into experimental use at the General Post Office, London, England. When an item of mail and a coin were inserted in the machine a red franking mark bearing the words 'Postage Paid' was impressed upon the face of the letter. By this means the use of a postage stamp was obviated. This particular machine, experimentally installed, was not notably successful and it was withdrawn from public use some months later.

The trial, nevertheless, was of some significance to philatelists and postmark collectors, for it may well have foreshadowed some of the vast and far-reaching changes which future years were to bring to the world's postal services. Already, to a substantial extent, the use of franking machines and printed devices by government departments and business concerns has superseded the use of adhesive postage stamps.

Today millions of postal packets are prepaid by the medium of franking machines and in the 1970s even the '10 letters a day' man may avail himself of a compact, modern mailing aid which puts the use of pre-cancelled electric metered mail well within his reach.

The first government to authorise the substitution of franked impressions for postage stamps was that of New Zealand. In 1904 an early model of Ernest Moss's postal franking machine was placed on trial and proved to be satisfactory.

Since that date enormous strides have been made towards the perfection of high speed machines capable of dispensing with the use of adhesive postage stamps. In 1920 Congress of the United States of America granted a licence to the Postage Meter Company for the use of an improved power-driven franking machine and in May 1922 the use of the American Pitney-Bowes machine was sanctioned by Britain's Postmaster-General. The first user was the giant Prudential Assurance Company at whose offices a model 'A' Pitney-Bowes postage meter was installed in September 1922, to be followed by a second machine a few months later. The original machine remained in daily use until September 1967 and was specially re-licensed by the British Post Office to service commemorative mail at a 50th anniversary ceremony at London's Dorchester Hotel in May 1972. In 1924 Roneo (later Roneo-Neopost) entered the field.

From these small beginnings the use of franking machines has developed to almost universal proportions completely revolutionising the despatch of mail in bulk. In America, in 1968, 74,000 postal franking machines were in operation. In Britain there was a sevenfold increase in their use between 1939 and 1964, by which time about 48,000 of them had been installed and by 1972 over 30 per cent of the total postage revenue in the UK derived from this source.

To visualise the next stage—whereby *individual* units of mail may be despatched by private persons without the use of adhesive stamps—is not difficult. By the early 1950s such an innovation had already passed the embryonic stage with the development in America of a coin-operated machine which permitted the insertion of one or all of four different denominations of coin, the values of which were registered in a cash dial in front of the machine. In this way the required postage value was dialled while the packets were fed successively into the posting aperture.

Developments such as these, including even more sophisticated innovations such as the setting up of Hovercraft mail services, the use of rocket mail facilities, the introduction of generic postmarks and the installation of Automatic Letter Facing equipment (as in Britain in 1957) suggest new and attractive prospects for the postmark collector. On the one hand he can record these changes by acquiring specimen imprints for his collection; on the other he can continue to harvest the postmarks of bygone days for the evidence they provide of past methods of mail-handling and their links with places and postal centres no longer in existence.

Another move, leading to the elimination of many individual town and village postmarks, has been the trend towards sophisticated mechanisation of mail handling methods. One result of this has been the appearance of what are sometimes termed 'generic' postmarks.

In America the first of these, NORTHERN VIRGINIA, introduced in 1968, covered a region representing several communities across the Potomac River from Washington, DC. In all, the Northern Virginia postmark embraced 61 post offices in the counties of Arlington, Fairfax, Prince William and London.

In the United Kingdom the first of the generic-type postmarks was FYLDE COAST, LANCS, introduced on 28 November 1966 for use on mails from the towns of Lytham St Annes, Blackpool, Cleveleys, Fleetwood and Poulton-le-Fylde and from villages on the peninsula between the Ribble and Wyre estuaries. It was soon to be followed by further group cancellations, including South Devon (introduced 28 July 1969), South West County Durham (5 January 1970), North Devon (9 March 1970), Exeter District (1 June 1970), Gloucestershire (7 October 1970), Medway (17 October 1970), Clwyd (1972) and others embracing specific areas.

Some people deplore the fact that because of these and similar changes many of the world's most interesting postal place-names and types of cancellations no longer exist: the post offices have closed and their postmarks are no longer issued. To subscribe to this view is to overlook the fact that *because* these offices are closed their postmarks, when they can be traced, may be among the really great 'finds' in a postmark collection. It is a thrill to track down the handstamps of some quaintly-named office that closed its doors

Selection of French pictorial slogans

for business half a century or more ago and if collectors can be pe suaded to retain and preserve the treasure they find, its value future generations will be considerable.

Whatever the effect of such innovations as postal franking an the introduction of generic-type postal cancellations two thin remain relatively certain. The first of these is that the value of carefully created collection of postmarks and postal history ma erial, as we know and understand these terms today, is far mo likely to be enhanced than reduced by the passage of years. Th second and perhaps most important point is that the relaxing pa time of collecting postmarks is rather like embarking on a person voyage of adventure and discovery. The traveller can never b quite sure where the journey will take him, or where it will en but he is sure to experience pleasure, surprise and a sense of dee enjoyment along the route.

Bibliography

GENERAL WORKS

Advanced Philatelic Research, Patrick Pearson (Arthur Barker Ltd, 1971)

Billig's Handbooks on Cancellations and Postmarks (HJMR, PO Box 308, North Miami, Florida, 33161, USA)

Carrying British Mail Overseas, Howard Robinson (George Allen & Unwin, 1964)

Christmas Story, A, C. W. Meredith and Cyril Kidd (R. C. Alcock Ltd, 1954)

GPO, E. T. Crutchley (Cambridge University Press, 1938)

History of the Post Office from its Establishment to 1836, The, Herbert Joyce (R. Bentley & Son, London, 1893)

History of the Post Office Packet Service, 1793–1815, Arthur H. Norway (Macmillan & Co, London, 1895)

Illustrated Handbook of New Zealand Registration Labels 1908–1965 Compiled by I. D. Campbell (The Postal History Society of New Zealand, 1965)

Mail Coach Men of the late 18th Century, The, Edmund Vale (David & Charles, Newton Abbot, 1967)

Mails, The, H. N. Soper (Universal Postal Frankers Ltd, London)

Maltese Cross Cancellations of the United Kingdom, R. C. Alcock and F. C. Holland (R. C. Alcock Ltd, 1971)

Penny Post 1680–1918, The, Frank Staff (Lutterworth Press, 1964)

Postmark Collecting, R. K. Forster (Stanley Paul & Co Ltd, London, 1960)

Postmark On A Letter, The, R. K. Forster (W. & R. Chambers Ltd, 1952)

Post Office, The, Olive Royston (Routledge & Kegan Paul, 1972)

Spoon Experiment 1853–1858, The, R. W. Willcocks and W. Bentley (1960)

Bibliography

Stamp Collector's Encyclopaedia, The, R. J. Sutton (Stanley Pau
Co Ltd, 1951, and later editions)
They Carried The Mail, Mathew J. Bowyer (Robert B. Lu
Washington, DC, 1972)

REGIONAL STUDIES

Bahamas Post Offices, Compiled by Gale J. Raymond (Bahan
Postal History Study Circle, 1962)
Britain's Post Office, Howard Robinson (Oxford University Pre
1953)
British Commemorative Handstamps 1970 (Superia Star
Company, Hove, Sussex)
British Postmarks, A Short History and Guide, R. C. Alcock a
F. C. Holland (R. C. Alcock Ltd, 1960)
British Post Office, The, C. F. Dendy Marshall (Oxford Univers
Press, 1926)
British Post Office Numbers (1844–1906), George Brumell (R.
Alcock Ltd, 1946)
Burma Postal History, D. Martin and G. Harris (Robson Lo
Ltd, London)
Christmas Island and its Postal History, (The Hawthorn Pre
Melbourne, 1953)
Durham Postal History, David Williams (Durham City Philate
Society, 1970)
English TPOs, Their History and Postmarks, C. W. Ward (19
Franklin's Guide to the Stamps of Papua and New Guinea, M
Franklin (A. H. & A. W. Reed, Sydney, 1970)
Greenland Postmarks Since 1938, Roland King-Farlow (1960)
History of British Postmarks, A, J. H. Daniels (L. Upcott (
London, 1898)
History of the Early Postmarks of the British Isles (to 1840), T
J. C. Hendy (L. Upcott Gill, London, 1905)
History of the Postmarks of the British Isles from 1840 to 18
J. C. Hendy (Stanley Gibbons Ltd, 1909)
Irish TPOs, Their History and Postmarks, C. W. Ward (1938)
Jamaica: Current Post Offices and Postmarks, S. G. Balley (Auth
Cardiff, Wales, 1968)

176

Japan: Scenery Cancellations, Dr H. K. Thompson (1956)

Krag Machine Cancellations, The, W. G. Stitt-Dibden and J. W. A. Lowder (The Postal History Society, 1960)

Local Posts of London (1680–1840), George Brumell (R. C. Alcock Ltd, 1939)

New South Wales Numeral Cancellations, Alan G. Brown and Hugh M. Campbell (The Royal Philatelic Society of Victoria, Australia, and Robson Lowe Ltd, London, 1963)

New Zealand Post Offices, R. M. Startup (The Postal History Society of New Zealand, 1967)

New Zealand Post Offices Past and Present, R. M. Startup (Laurie Franks Ltd, Christchurch, New Zealand, 1960)

Norona's General Catalog US Postmarks, (1935 and 1946)

Obliterations et Marques Postales des Etats-Unis, Michael Zareski, (Paris, France)

Postage Stamps and Postal History of the Bahamas, Harold G. D. Gisburn (Stanley Gibbons Ltd, London, 1950)

Postal Cancellations of London 1840–1940, The, H. C. Westley, (Johnson, London, 1950)

Postal History Map of Britain, (John Bartholomew & Son Ltd, 1970)

Postal History of the Antarctic 1904–1909, The, Richard W. Bagshawe and John Goldup (Scott Polar Research Institute, Cambridge, England, 1951)

Postal History of Barnet, Hertfordshire and Surrounding Districts 1642–1971, Roy Henderson (Barnet & District Philatelic Society, 1971)

Postal History of Huddersfield, The, Eric Buckley (Yorkshire Postal History Society, 1968)

Postal History of the British West Indies, Introduction to, L. E. Britnor (British West Indies Study Circle, 1959)

Postal History of the Isle of Man to 1867, The, Ronald Ward and Brian Leece (The Postal History Society, 1969)

Postal History of Nova Scotia and New Brunswick 1754–1867, The, (Sissons Publications Ltd, Toronto, Canada, 1964)

Postal History of Sweden, The, J. Alfred Birch (The Postal History Society)

Postal History of Western Australia 1829–1901, The, George E. Owen (The Hawthorn Press, Melbourne, 1959)

Postal History of Yukon Territory, The, R. G. Woodall, (Wimborn
Dorset, 1964)

Postal Markings of Maryland 1766–1855, Powers (1960)

Postal Markings of Spain, Theo Van Dam (1965)

Postmark Slogans of Great Britain, The, George Brumell (R. (
Alcock Ltd, 1938)

Postmarks of British New Guinea and Papua to 1942, The, Hamilto
Croaker (The Hawthorn Press, Melbourne, 1956)

Postmarks of Great Britain and Ireland 1661–1940, The, R. (
Alcock and F. C. Holland (R. C. Alcock Ltd, Cheltenham, 194
with supplements)

Postmarks of the British Isles, George Brumell (1930)

Post Offices and Postal Cancellations of Fiji, H. M. Campbell (Th
Hawthorn Press, Melbourne, 1957)

Post Offices in Scotland, compiled by J. R. Henderson (Th
Scottish Postmark Group, Edinburgh, 1966)

Posts of Essex, The, L. J. Johnson (The Postal History Society, 196
Queensland Numeral Cancellations, Harry S. Porter (The Hawthor
Press, Melbourne, 1954)

Saffron Walden: Some Aspects of the Postal History of an Esse
Market Town, M. V. D. Champness (East Anglia Postal Histor
Study Circle, 1970)

St Lucia: Current Post Offices and Postmarks, S. G. Balley (Cardif
Wales, 1968)

Scotland in Stamps; A Guide to the Postal History, Postage Stamp
and Postmarks of Scotland, C. W. Hill, (Impulse Book
Aberdeen, Scotland)

Scots Local Cancellations, C. W. Meredith (R. C. Alcock Ltd, 195c
Scottish TPOs, Their History and Postmarks, C. W. Ward (1947
Slogan Cancellations of the Republic of Ireland 1922–1959, F. I
Dixon (1959)

Slogan Postmarks of the United Kingdom, C. R. H. Parsons an
G. R. Pearson (1965, with supplements)

Slogan Postmarks of the United Kingdom, C. R. H. Parsons, C. C
Peachey, G. R. Pearson (G. R. Pearson, 42 Corrance Roac
London, SW2 5RH, 1972)

Special Event Postmarks of the United Kingdom, G. R. Pearso
(1963)

Bibliography

Stamford Postal History, W. G. Stitt Dibden and L. Tebbutt (The Postal History Society, 1961)

Stamps and Postal History of Sarawak, The, W. R. Forrester-Wood (1971)

Stamps and Postal History of the Channel Islands, William Newport (William Heinemann Ltd, London, 1972)

Union of South Africa: List of Post and Telegraph Offices (1912) Dr. T. B. Berry (Philatelic Society of Johannesburg)

US County and Postmaster Postmarks, Dr Howard K. Thompson (179 pp about 1,000 illustrations)

Welsh Post Towns Before 1840, Michael Scott Archer (Phillimore & Co Ltd, Chichester, Sussex, 1970)

OFFICIAL PUBLICATIONS AND GUIDES

Dictionnaire des Bureaux de Poste, in two volumes (Universal Postal Union, Berne, Switzerland, 1951)

Directory of Post Offices (United States Post Office Department, Washington, DC)

Liste des Numeros Postaux (Swiss Post Offices)

London Post Offices and Streets (HM Stationery Office)

Nomenclature Internationale des Bureaux de Poste (UPU, Berne, 1968)

Post Office Guide, Commonwealth of Australia

Post Office Guide (Postmaster-General, East African Posts and Telecommunications Administration)

Post Office Guide (Federal Government of Nigeria)

Post Office Guide (Republic of Ireland) (Stationery Office, Dublin)

Post Offices in the Republic of South Africa

Post Offices in the United Kingdom (HM Stationery Office)

Post Offices in the United Kingdom and The Irish Republic (HM Stationery Office)

Statistique des Services Postaux (Universal Postal Union, 1969)

ASSOCIATED SUBJECTS

Airmails 1870–1970, James Mackay (B. T. Batsford Ltd, London, 1971)

Bibliography

Camp Postmarks of the United Kingdom, R. A. Kingston (Forces Postal History Society, 1971)

Collecting Postal History, Prince Dimitry Kandaouroff (Peter Lowe, London, 1973)

Cover Collecting, James Mackay (Philatelic Publishers Ltd, 1968)

Handstruck Postage Stamps of the Empire, Robson Lowe (Herbert Joseph, Ltd, 1937)

Haste, Post, Haste!, George Walker (G. Harrap & Co Ltd, 1938)

History of Wreck Covers, A, Adrian E. Hopkins (3rd edition, Robson Lowe Ltd, 1970)

Penny Postage Centenary, (Postal History Society, London)

Picton's Priced Catalogue of British Pictorial Postcards and Post-marks 1894–1939, compiled by M. R. Hewlett (BPH Publications Ltd, 1971)

Picture Postcard: A Collector's Guide to the Golden Age, The, T. and V. Holt (MacGibbon & Kee, 1971)

Picture Postcard and its Origins, The, Frank Staff (Lutterworth Press, 1966)

Postal History and Postmarks of the Franco-Prussian War, W. Bentley (1955)

Stamps of Great Britain (Part 1), J. B. Seymour (Royal Philatelic Society, London, 1934)

Story of Great Britain and her Stamps, The, James Mackay, (Philatelic Publishers Ltd, London, 1967)

Tale of the Kicking Mule, The, Lee H. Cornell (Published in Wichita, Kansas, USA)

Index

Index